His Grandson's Tales to Beelzebub

His Grandson's Tales to Beelzebub

David Thayer

✠ Universal Christ Church Press ✠

Cover photo of the Whirlpool Galaxy (M51) courtesy of NASA and the Space Telescope Science Institute.

This book was prepared with Microsoft® Publisher 2010 running on Microsoft Windows® 7 Professional. PDFs for CreateSpace were done with Adobe Acrobat X.

The main text is set in 11-point Adobe Minion Pro,™ on 14-point leading. Chapter titles are 22-point Caslon Open Face. Quotations in chapter headings are 8-point Lucida® Calligraphy. Drop caps are 66-point Augsburger Initials.

Manufactured in the United States of America
Printed by CreateSpace, an Amazon company

Published by the Universal Christ Church Press
An imprint of Rapidsoft Press   SAN 299-5840
Sarasota, Florida

First printing: 1988
Second printing: 1999
Third printing: 2004
Fourth printing: 2007
Fifth printing: 2014

Publisher's Cataloging in Publication Data

Thayer, David
   His Grandson's Tales to Beelzebub
      1. Mysticism
      2. Religion
      I. Title

ISBN 978-0-9663909-3-3

DID NOT WANT to write this book. I had two very good reasons for not wanting to. First, I knew I could not write it. Second, I didn't know enough to write it even were I capable of doing so. None of this has changed. Nevertheless, the book does exist (unless all the following pages are blank. Have you looked? Better do it now, before it's too late!), and this simple fact requires some sort of explanation.

For years I went about my affairs trusting that tomorrow I should somehow come by the competence and knowledge necessary to write this book. Then one midsummer's night, in the wee hours of the morning, the Life Force of the universe grabbed hold of me and shook me until my brains rattled, telling me bluntly: "Tomorrow is Never!"

And so it is.

Reluctantly, I sat down to begin my impossible task. I started writing a book I was incapable of writing. If you are looking forward to finding out how I overcame such formidable obstacles you're going to be disappointed. I did not overcome them; they overcame me. I *was* incapable of writing this book, just as I had suspected all along.

So how come the book exists?

That's easy—I didn't write it. Beelzebub's grandson dictated it to me and I just wrote it down. The vast reservoir of knowledge that supplied what you will find here was tapped by him, not me. I've been granted but one small spigot that drips slowly, like a punctured tree trunk oozing sap.

Make no mistake about it: these are mystic teachings. Here you will find wisdom that transcends the limitations of space and time, penetrates the far reaches of Eternity, and draws your mind out of its normal habitat. You may find some of the concepts shocking. That's the whole idea. But be of good cheer, my friend. Our only aim is to lift up your consciousness to unforeseen heights.

I hope you will have as much fun reading these stories as I had in writing them down. But even more than that I pray that what you learn might start you, too, down the same path where once passed Beelzebub's grandson.

David Thayer
Las Cruces,
New Mexico
July 1988

Prologue

OLELY BY VIRTUE of amazingly good fortune have I come by the collection of stories comprising this little book. Had I not met Beelzebub's grandson I could never have written any of this. So I should tell you what little I know about this unusual young man who claims as his grandfather a man named Beelzebub.

WE FIRST MET in the foothills of the Organ Mountains, deep inside southern New Mexico where a long finger of the Chihuahuan Desert pokes northward up the valley of the Rio Grande. It was late in the summer and recent cloudbursts from the final efforts of the southwestern monsoon had brought out wild flowers in profusion. I was walking along a trail in back of a large rock formation called *La Cueva* when I noticed a young man on the hillside above me picking and immediately eating every wild mushroom he could find. Fearing he might eat some kind of mushroom that could do him in, I climbed the hill. I found him eating some small silvery mushrooms he had just picked from a cow dropping. I didn't much notice his appearance, because he is really a rather nondescript person. He looked about thirty or so, tall, slender build, sandy colored hair with streaks of gray at the temples.

I got right to the point.

"Say," I began, "aren't you afraid of eating a poisonous one?"

He smiled. "No, Beelzebub wouldn't let me."

His answer floored me.

"Beelzebub?" I echoed. "You mean Old Scratch?"

I began to look around a bit apprehensively. He laughed.

"No, Beelzebub is my grandfather." He said this in such a matter-of-fact manner that I searched his face to see if he might be putting me on. It was then I first noticed his eyes; they are the only really striking thing about the man. His direct gaze seemed to penetrate right to my bone, as though he had x-ray vision like Superman. And looking into his eyes, I discovered, is a trip. I had a sudden, irrational feeling of vertigo, as though I were peering down a very deep mineshaft. I quickly broke my eyes away, pretending to look for his grandfather. He watched me with amusement.

"Oh, he's not here, but he takes care of me anyhow."

Deciding he was some kind of nut, I ended our conversation. Though I believed I would never see him again, I couldn't seem to get him out of my mind. I felt strangely disappointed the next time I passed that way and he wasn't there. Then one day a few weeks later I went up to *La Cueva* on a hunch, having thought about the man for some time that day. Much to my surprise he was there, sitting cross-legged on a rock. I pretended not to have noticed him and continued walking along the trail.

Half an hour later, after I had gotten up my nerve, I went back and found him still sitting in the same position. He didn't appear to notice me at all, so I did likewise. I sat down about fifteen feet away, as if I were alone. After five minutes or so he spoke without moving anything but his lips.

"You want me to tell you, don't you." A statement of fact.

"Tell me what?" I asked, floored again.

"All the stories I told Beelzebub when I got back."

"Back?"

"Yes. My grandfather sent me out into the world to find myself, as he put it. When I got back, I told him all about it."

"And?"

"He told me I was mad." I raised my eyebrows. He smiled— he seemed amused with most of my reactions—and added, "Coming from him, it was a great compliment."

"Oh," was all I could reply. But I was already interested enough to come back and talk to this young paradox week after week (he wouldn't come to me, I had to go to him). At first I just listened, but after that I began bringing a portable cassette recorder. From those recordings I wrote this book. When I first brought the recorder, he seemed pleased but not surprised. He said he knew I had to write this book, that it was "my work," just as it was "his work" to tell me the stories.

The stories he told me speak for themselves, but I should add one or two details about this strange person before going on to them. For one thing, he does excellent impersonations of Walt Disney characters—you know, Goofy, Mickey Mouse, Donald Duck. Strangely, I never saw him do an impersonation of anyone else. He is also a master juggler. I have often seen him juggling fifteen or twenty balls, and I once saw him juggle no less than forty-six small plastic eggs. I found out since that this is impossible. The world record for juggling balls is something like a dozen. Yet I saw him do it.

It's far from the strangest thing about him.

Metamorphosis

Born of the Ancient of Days he came,
Out of the dusty hills of Natzrat
To the river of Dan, with waters renewing

At the hands of the Baptist,
The waters closed over a son of man:
Yeshua ben Yosef, son of the carpenter

The waters reopened to a new dawn,
The heavens split: the sun with a new sun,
Son of the Father born anew

Forged in the wilderness furnace,
He emptied himself of self, for us,
Revealing the Son light for all to see

Through the world of man he passed,
And we beheld his glory, uncovered now,
Reflecting the light of the Most High

But in our ignorance we would not know him,
Nor in our sorrow could we receive him;
So we sacrificed him to the darkness

And the darkness swallowed him,
But it could not hold him—
A blaze of glory ripped him free

Released as Son shine, waxing bright,
Spirit pure, hand of the Father reaching out—
To those who have eyes to see

Tarries he now by the still waters,
His true love to receive with joy—
Perchance he awaits again for thee

Perchance he awaits once more for thee . . .

O, call back yesterday,
bid time return.

—William Shakespeare,
Richard II, Act 3, Scene 2

1

The Train

had not the faintest idea what I was going to do when my grandfather sent me out into the world. "You are thrice seven, O son of my daughter," he said to me, "and it is high time you found out who you are. Go out into the world and seek yourself. Take nothing with you and spend no time thinking about what you will eat or where you will sleep. Do not even think about what you are doing or should be doing—as you might fancy it. Instead, at all times follow this one rule only: Never try to do anything or be anything, but always *be here now*. If you don't know what you're doing you will always be able to do it, even if it is impossible." This was all he gave me with which to go forth and conquer the world. When I protested that it was not enough, he said he had already taught me everything he knew.

"No way!" I exploded. "I know next to nothing!"

"Of course," he replied cheerfully, "you didn't understand any of what I told you." He anticipated my next question: "But you know all of it anyway. What you require is hidden in the stories I have told you. It will come back to you when you need to know. Then you will understand."

I quickly realized further protests would be useless and left. For most of that first day I felt frustrated and angry. Frustrated because I had no idea of what I was about, and angry that my own grandfather had sent me on this impossible quest.

I must confess I completely ignored his advice to me. All day long I worried about what I was going to eat and where I would be able to sleep. As a result—so I later discovered—I went to sleep hungry that night, huddled up against the side of a barn. It was a chilly night and I was so cold that I couldn't get to sleep for a long time. At length I fell into a deep sleep despite the chattering of my teeth.

I awoke to a glorious sunrise. I stood up and stretched this way and that, luxuriating in the warmth of the sunshine as it drove the stiffness and aches from my body. I marveled at the freshness of the early morning, the stirring of the creatures, the singing of birds, the beauty of it all. I had spent perhaps the better part of half an hour this way when I heard a deep male voice say, "You!" Turning, I saw a short, swarthy man smoking a pipe and holding an axe in his hand.

"I sprained my wrist," he said, "and can't use this axe. If you'll chop some wood for me, I'll share my breakfast with you."

I realized then how hungry I was and quickly agreed to his proposition. The man used the wood I chopped to make a fire in a pot-bellied stove, on which he prepared a hearty breakfast for the two of us.

While we were eating I told the man my story, which was, of course, quite short at that point. He took pity on me—or so I believed at the time—and gave me a down jacket together with a generous supply of beef jerky. He said the jacket once belonged to his son who had been killed in the war. We parted friends although I never learned his name.

MUCH LATER THAT DAY I suddenly realized there might be some connection between forgetting my predicament while watching the sunrise and the unexpected windfall of breakfast and provisions that had followed. Although I could see no relationship of cause and effect between those events or between the contrary events of the day before, I soon resolved to try following my grandfather's advice in the future. From then on I made every effort to concentrate on what I was doing at the moment. While walking I tried to do a good job of walking. When talking, I concentrated only on talking. Even though I found myself slipping into old habits from time to time, these relapses were useful because they confirmed the relationship between concentration and results many times. Eventually, I no longer had any reason to doubt the truth of Beelzebub's words. We do reap the results of our thoughts just as surely as we reap the fruits of our actions.

Early that afternoon I stopped at a small cafe for a drink of water. The proprietor, a kindly little old man in his seventies, gave me a delicious lunch consisting of a bowl of soup, a sandwich, and a cup of mint tea. It had been ordered, he explained, by a customer who was abruptly called away. He had already eaten, he added, and if he did not give it to me he would have to throw it away. I soon found that I could expect this sort of thing to happen so long as I maintained right concentration. Should I fall into worry or despair, however, good fortune seemed to vanish from the face of the earth.

You will understand that I told none of these things to my grandfather upon my return. By then I knew he would find them irrelevant. The first tale I told him began later that second day, as dusk settled over the land. I had shared dinner with a strange man, big but quite gentle with an imposing black beard and hair that fell to his shoulders. We nibbled on my beef jerky and some dried fruit, which the man had in his knapsack. Later, he prepared two cups of tea that were most unusual. The tea bags appeared to be homemade, but instead of tea leaves they contained small squares of what looked like paper, about one centimeter on a side. He used no heat to prepare the tea, yet as soon as he had placed the tea bags in our cups the water began to boil furiously as if heated from below. As soon as the boiling stopped we drank the tea, which I found to be just the right temperature for drinking. It had an unusual, oriental flavor and was quite tasty. Afterwards, we set off down the road.

We had walked perhaps a kilometer or two when darkness began to overtake us. As we walked into a dark grove of trees I suddenly became aware of a man standing in the road in front of us.

"You're late," the man said.

Thinking the man was addressing my bearded friend, I turned to see how he would reply. Much to my surprise he was nowhere in sight. I was alone with this stranger.

"I am the Conductor," he said, sensing my discomfort. "I have been waiting for you."

I was speechless but did manage to come forward to get a closer look at the man. His wrinkled skin and snow-white hair told of many years. Although about my height and build, he was so bent over as to appear shorter than I. He was wearing some kind of uniform and a cap like the ones train conductors wear.

"Let me have your bags," he said. When I told him I had none, he looked obviously relieved and told me to follow him. I really wanted to run away from there as fast as I could, but something in the back of my mind told me I had better do as the fellow asked. Barely able to see my way, I just followed the Conductor, who seemed to know where he was going.

We had walked only a few meters into the woods when we came upon a large dark object, which I finally recognized as a railroad car. I could see tracks underneath it, but only the one car. I did, however, notice a humming sound like a large locomotive idling and a sort of hissing sound like compressed air escaping. I could discern no source for either of these sounds.

I followed the Conductor into the car, which was empty. He bade me sit down in one of the seats. Since all the window shades were rolled down, making it impossible to see out, I reached for the shade next to my seat. Before I could touch it the Conductor stopped me, saying I should not draw the shade until the train was moving. I began to think the whole thing was ridiculous. There was no train, so far as I could see, and this was just a silly game. The Conductor, I decided, was some kind of nut and I had better humor him.

A sudden jolt interrupted my thoughts. Immediately afterwards I felt a gentle pressure like a train slowly gathering speed. Despite my doubts the car was moving. After a few minutes the train seemed to have reached a steady speed with only a slight swaying motion and the occasional click-clack of metal wheels to disturb the quiet. The Conductor came up the aisle and told me I could pull up my window shade now if I wanted to. With much curiosity as to what I should see, I started to pull the shade up only to be jolted to the depths of my being. It was broad daylight outside, and instead of the woods where we had started out I saw only broad grassy meadows with horses and cows grazing.

"How did we get here?" I asked, astounded.

"In eight minutes," replied the Conductor, looking at his watch.

That was hardly an answer to my question, I thought to myself, but I was almost afraid to ask anything more. So I kept quiet for a while, looking out the window and trying to understand what kind of situation I had gotten myself into.

Shortly afterwards we pulled into a station. I noticed a sign that read "Homestead." The train stopped for a minute or so. Although several people were standing on the platform talking with each other, so far as I could tell no one either got on or off the train. We got under way again, and while I was still trying to sort things out in my head, the Conductor reappeared.

"Did you notice the station we stopped at?"

"Yes. Homestead, wasn't it?"

"Quite so," replied the Conductor. "Too bad it's gone."

"Gone? What do you mean by 'gone'?"

"This train only goes one way. Once we've passed a place, it's gone forever."

"No it's not," I retorted. "It's most certainly not gone. All I'd have to do is get off the train, go back to where it was, and there it would be—big as life."

The Conductor broke into a broad grin upon hearing these words. I felt strangely flushed, as though I were a little boy back in grade school and the teacher had just said, "That's very good!"

"Yes, so it would," said the Conductor, still grinning from ear to ear. "You'll do quite nicely, I'm sure."

"Say, what is this all about, anyway?" I asked, beginning to feel a bit nettled. "That town we passed—Homestead—where is it? I've never heard of it. In fact, I've never seen any of this land before."

The Conductor frowned and pulled out his watch. He scrutinized it carefully, and his brow furrowed over as though he were figuring something in his head.

"Homestead," he said, as if announcing it. "It's at exactly two twenty-two."

"What kind of answer is that?" I protested.

"Accurate," he replied, "very accurate." Then he smiled, turned on his heel, and began to walk out of the car.

"Wait a minute," I called as he headed to the door. Frantically trying to think of a sensible question to ask, I blurted out: "What time is it, then?"

"Now," he replied. "It's always *now*." He paused in the doorway, looking at me as if expecting another question.

"Well, then, *where* are we?"

"Glad you asked; thought you never would." He broke into his broad grin again, pulled out his pocket watch, and announced:

"Two thirty. We're at two thirty on the dot."

Without another word he disappeared. I couldn't believe it. I ask him what time it is, and he tells me now; I ask him where we are, and he tells me the time. Following him through the door to ask another question, I found myself in a cubicle about three feet deep running the width of the car. Except for the door I had come in through, the walls were perfectly smooth without any hint of a door or other way of going further. The Conductor was not there. Stunned, I made my way back to my seat and sat down, my head spinning. My whole world seemed to be disintegrating. My grandfather had told me some rather strange stories, but nothing so bizarre as what was happening now.

A sudden lurching of the railroad car interrupted my thoughts. I was thrown against the window and my head hit the window shade, causing it to suddenly roll up the rest of the way. It was still going *zinggg* the way shades do after abruptly rolling up when my attention was drawn to the scene outside the window. We were no longer in the countryside but had come into a village. At first I thought perhaps we were in Mexico because I saw a rather large woman in a bright red dress eating a taco she had evidently purchased from a sidewalk vendor. However, a sign on a nearby building read *Wilson Post Office*. We were not in Mexico.

Then it struck me that the train was no longer moving. At least, it didn't appear to be as things were not moving past outside. However, the swaying and clicking continued as before, giving the odd illusion that the train was speeding on its way while not moving at all. I watched, fascinated, while the woman in red ate her taco, bought and ate another one, and went on her way. I watched a young boy set up a shoe shine stand and sit down to await customers. After a while a man came and took down the sign over the post office. He put up a new one reading *Hanover Post Office*. I watched a few people stop for a shoe shine and several others purchase food from the sidewalk vendor. I reflected that these activities should have consumed an hour or so, yet I felt that not more than fifteen minutes had passed since the train stopped.

The Conductor's voice interrupted my reveries.

"Nice day, isn't it?" he asked pleasantly.

I just stared at him. Where the devil had he come from? For that matter, where had he gone? Before I could ask one of the questions that were popping into my mind, he asked me one.

"Where's Wilson?"

"Why, right here, right out there." I pointed out the window.

"No it isn't," said the Conductor. "That's Hanover."

"But they just changed the name," I protested.

"Indeed they did. But where is Wilson?" he persisted.

"Oh, I see what you mean—Wilson's gone. They changed the name to Hanover, and it's gone. There isn't any Wilson now."

"Quite so; there isn't any Wilson now," the Conductor agreed, but before I could feel relieved he added: "But that doesn't mean it's gone, does it?"

"Of course it does," I insisted. "Once something's gone, it's gone for good. Time only goes one way; once it's past, it's gone."

"Speak for yourself," said the Conductor. "Why couldn't you just get off the train and go back to Wilson, just as you said you could go back to Homestead?"

"That's different. Homestead is a place. You can go back to a place, but you can't go back to another time. It just doesn't work that way."

"Speak for yourself," he said again.

"What do you mean? I suppose you could go back to Wilson if you wanted to?"

"My time is mine, and your time is yours. Let me take care of my time, and you mind your own."

I wasn't getting anywhere, so I tried to change the subject.

"Why has the train stopped, anyway?"

"It hasn't," came the reply, "you have." I started to protest, but he cut me off, saying, "Before you get yourself any more mixed up, I strongly suggest you take a walk in the aisle. You need to clear your head."

With that, the Conductor turned and walked away again. I got up to follow, but remembering what had happened the last time I tried to follow him I thought better of the idea and turned to go back to my seat. As I did so I chanced to look out the window, and what I saw froze me in my tracks. The scene was completely different from when I had been seated. I saw the same town, so recently changed into Hanover, but I was seeing it in an entirely different way. In the first place, the train was obviously moving and not standing still as I had thought. But it was moving in a totally unfamiliar way. If I caught sight of any object and turned my head to follow it as it fell behind the train, it looked exactly the same until it was out of sight. Then, if I turned back and looked straight out the window to where the object had been in the first place, it was still there—only it might have changed.

I first noticed this while watching the shoeshine boy. I had fixed my gaze on him and followed him as he receded into the distance. He remained as if frozen, one hand in the air holding his brush, the other stretched out to receive payment for the shoeshine he had just finished. When I lost sight of him in the distance, I looked back straight out the window and there he was—just putting the change back in his pocket as his customer walked away down the street. Fascinated now, I fixed my eyes on the clock in front of the bank building, which stood on the corner next to the post office. It read exactly five past eleven. I watched it for some time until I lost sight of it, too, and the hands never moved. When I looked back, the clock was still there. But it read six after eleven now.

I felt the hair raising up on the back of my neck. This was really spooky! On a hunch, I looked up ahead of the train. Sure enough, there was the same village, the same bank, the same clock. Only now the clock read seven after eleven. And there was a pigeon sitting on top of the clock. Quickly I moved back into my seat. As soon as I sat down, the scene was entirely normal again. All sensation of motion vanished, and if I looked one way or the other all I saw was what was there, just as in everyday life.

I looked at the clock. It read six after eleven and about thirty seconds. I watched it carefully. There was no pigeon. The second hand clicked its way around the face of the clock. Fifteen seconds to go, ten seconds . . . suddenly a large pigeon fluttered down and perched on top of the clock, preening its feathers. I began to freak out. My hair must have been standing straight up.

I stood up and sat down a number of times to verify that this was what was causing the difference between the views I was seeing. It was. I saw a young girl walking down the street towards the corner in front of me. A car was coming down the alley toward the same street. It was moving quite fast, but the girl couldn't see it from where she was walking. I raised up and looked ahead. There I could see the nose of the car poking out of the alley and the girl in mid-air, her body grotesquely sprawled out like a rag doll, suspended motionless. I sat down and gestured wildly out the window, but although she seemed to look right at me the girl did not notice. Then the car hurtled out of the alley and sent the girl flying through the air. She landed all crumpled up in a heap on the other side of the street, blood trickling from the corner of her mouth. She didn't move. A man with a bag rushed out of a doorway and ran over to the girl. He held her wrist briefly in his hand, reached out and closed her eyes. He covered her body with his jacket and went back inside. In a few minutes an ambulance came and took away the dead girl.

I sat there for a long time, my mind racing, searching for some meaning to all of these things I had seen. Finally it came to me. After I thought of it, it seemed quite simple, really. Time—at least here—wasn't what we supposed it to be at all. This train I was on was travelling through time the way most trains pass through the countryside. Here, different times were like different places. The future was ahead of the train, the past was behind it. You saw *now* when you looked straight out the window, or when you were sitting down. The things in the past weren't gone after all, they just could not be seen anymore, at least not while sitting down.

A few minutes later I noticed that everyone in the village seemed to be moving in slow motion. The hands on the clock were hardly moving. On a hunch I stood up, and, sure enough, the train had slowed down to a crawl. Then there was a slight lurch and a feeling of acceleration, and soon the train was moving right along. Soon it sped up so that it was really zipping through the, er, different times. When I sat down again, everything moved frantically. It was like watching an old movie. I realized that the speed of the train was what determined the rate of time passing in the scenes I was watching while I was sitting down.

Sometime later the Conductor returned, as I knew he would. I told him what I believed I had learned. He seemed pleased, but he told me that I needed to take one more step.

"You've got to realize that what you're seeing is real. This isn't just a show I'm putting on for you. The train isn't doing it, it's just happening. You're seeing things you could never see before. Nothing has changed except you."

"You mean time is like a train we're on that takes us into the future? And the only reason we think the past is gone is because we don't know how to get off the train?"

"Something like that," he replied.

"But where's the train?"

"It's right in there," said the Conductor, pointing at my head.

Without waiting for any reply from me, he reached up and pulled on a cord that ran along the roof of the car. There was a lurch and the train began to slow down rapidly. He saw the puzzled look on my face and explained.

"End of the line."

The train did not stop. Instead it reversed directions. It was going backwards now. In a few minutes I watched the ambulance back up to the curb and deposit the young girl's body on the sidewalk. Then the man with the bag ran rapidly backwards out of a building, opened the girl's eyes, felt her wrist, and ran backwards into another building. Blood was running up the girl's face and into the corner of her mouth. Seconds later her body abruptly flew through the air, hit a car that was going backwards into the alley, and then she was walking backwards down the sidewalk.

The train must have sped up then because things began to move faster and faster. I saw the fat lady in the red dress un-eating her taco. Every time she put it to her mouth she deposited another bite into an empty place until the taco was whole again. Then she handed it back to the vendor, who took it apart and put all the ingredients back where they had come from. Before long the hands on the clock in front of the bank were whirling backwards—the hour hand was moving like a second hand, the minute hand was a blur, and the second hand was going so fast I couldn't see it at all. I began to feel dizzy, as though I might black out. I looked around for the Conductor but he was nowhere to be seen. I wanted to ask him to stop the train so I could catch my breath. It was the last thing I could remember before passing out.

✧   ✧   ✧

I WOKE UP SUDDENLY, only to find myself in a clearing in the forest. It was morning. Nearby I saw a wooden railroad car standing on a section of rusty, ancient-looking track perhaps thirty meters long; the car was dilapidated and falling apart. I was alone.

I got up and shook my head to clear it out, but I could not shake the memory of what I had seen on the train. It was too real to dismiss as a dream.

I heard a voice, and going in the direction of the sound I soon came to the road I had been on last night. There was my bearded friend, sitting by the side of the road cross-legged, chanting some kind of mantra.

"Good morning!" he said when he saw me. "Did you have a nice trip?"

"How did you know?" I asked, astounded that he should have had any inkling of what I had gone through the night before.

"It was the tea," he announced. "It always does that. I think I gave you a bit too much."

Tea! Did he really expect me to believe that?

Food for Thought

Santa Spirita, breather, life,
Beyond the light, lighter than light,
Beyond the flames of hell, joyous, leaping easily above hell,
Beyond Paradise, perfumed solely with mine own perfume,
Including all life on earth, touching, including God, including Saviour
        and Satan,
Ethereal, pervading all, (for without me what were all? what were God?)
Essence of forms, life of the real identities, permanent, positive,
        (namely the unseen,)
Life of the great round world, the sun and stars, and of man,
        I, the general soul,
Here the square finishing, the solid, I the most solid,
Breathe my breath also through these songs.

                —"Chanting the Square Deific," stanza 4, 1865–66

I do not doubt that I am limitless, and that the universes are limitless,
        in vain I try to think how limitless,
I do not doubt that the orbs and the systems of orbs play their swift sports
        through the air on purpose,
            and that I shall one day be eligible to do as much as they,
            and more than they,
…
I do not doubt interiors have their interiors, and exteriors have their
        exteriors,
            and that the eyesight has another eyesight, and the hearing
            another hearing, and the voice another voice,
…
(Did you think Life was so well provided for, and Death, the purport of
        all Life, is not well provided for?)
…
I do not think Life provides for all and for Time and Space,
        but I believe Heavenly Death provides for all.

                —from "Assurances," 1856

                both from *Leaves of Grass* by Walt Whitman

To see a World in a grain of Sand
And a Heaven in a Wild flower,
Hold Infinity in the palm of your hand
And Eternity in an hour.

—William Blake,
"Auguries of Innocence,"
in *Poems from the Pickering Manuscript*

2

The Seer

My bearded friend and I kept company for several days after my strange train ride, and we became quite open with each other. Soon I felt secure enough to divulge to him the details of my trip with the Conductor. My companion mused in silence for quite a while after I finished telling him my story—so long that I began to wonder if he was ever going to comment about it. Finally, he turned and said:

"You know, man, he was only trying to turn you on to something heavy. Like, time is relative. Each of us carries his own clock around with him, but just because we're tied to it doesn't mean it's the only one there is."

"Yes," I replied, "I see what you mean. But I have a feeling there is a lot more to it than just that."

"Sure there is. He was showing you that there's spaces where time is a place and not time anymore."

"That's it!" I exclaimed. "That's exactly what I mean. That train got into different times by moving into different spaces. It had nothing to do with time on the train. And when the train went backwards, all the old times were still there to see."

We talked about it some more, but we never succeeded in putting my experience into words any better than that. Early the next afternoon we parted company. But before we did, my friend gave me some advice.

"You seem like you really want to learn about things, man," he began, "so I'm going to turn you on to something else that's really heavy, too. After you pass through the next town you're going to see a little white house tucked way back on the top of a hill. You can just barely see it from the road. When you find it, walk up there and sit on the doorstep. Don't knock on the door or anything, just sit there. If the old boy who lives there wants to see you, he'll invite you in. And I'm betting that he will. I'll bet he's waiting for you, right now. Know what I mean?"

"Is this old man a friend of yours?"

"He sure is! Man, I've been there a few times. And I'm telling you right now, it sure is worth the trip!"

"All right!" This was beginning to sound interesting. "If he's a friend of yours I'll try to see him, for sure!"

I WENT ON MY WAY with renewed confidence, satisfied that at least this old man didn't sound as weird as the Conductor. I found the place my friend had told me about quite easily. After climbing the steep hillside to the little white house I sat down as instructed, tired and winded. I had not been there ten minutes when the front door creaked open behind me. I turned and saw a wizened, elfin little face peering at me through the doorway.

"Be you the grandson?" he asked.

I was immediately taken aback. Did he know my grandfather? Or think I was his own grandson? I decided just to play along.

"Yes," I replied.

"All right, then, don't just set there a-bakin' in the sun! Come on inside and set you down."

I did as he asked and soon found myself inside one of the quaintest homes I have ever seen. Everything in it was small and antique, just like the man who lived in it. If my friend had told me the old man was an elf, I think I should have believed it at that point. But the little man quickly put me at ease, serving me tea and crackers and plying me with questions about where I was going and where I had been. I wasn't sure I should tell him about the Conductor and his train, so I didn't. Despite this omission, the old man showed great interest in me and my pilgrimage.

We passed the afternoon in what seemed to be idle chit-chat, until I chanced to state that I believed the world and everything in it was made out of atoms.

"Atoms?" he queried. "What do you know about 'em? Have you ever seen one?"

"Of course not," I replied, "nobody has. They're too small to see."

"Don't count on it, sonny, don't count on it. I'll bet you've never seen the whole universe inside of an eggshell, either. Well, don't pay it no never mind, you will soon enough."

I pressed him for details as to what he meant, but all he would say was to be patient and in due time I would see what I wanted to. There wasn't anything I could do anyway, so I took his advice and bode my time. But despite my outward calm I was beginning to get an uneasy feeling that this was going to turn out something like the train and its Conductor.

I soon forgot my uneasiness when the old man served supper. It was a delicious meal, but one thing puzzled me: when had the old man prepared it? He had been talking with me for most of the afternoon. I didn't ask him about it, however, as I was half afraid he would say that the meal had prepared itself. I was getting used to having strange ideas thrown at me.

After dinner the old man served some kind of liqueur. It was very dark green and thick, with a strong pungent odor. It was mouthwatering, however, and it warmed my gullet nicely on the way down. When I asked him what it was, he smiled and told me it was "nectar of the gods." He added, "It'll open your eyes, all right," and chuckled. I nodded, thinking he meant the liqueur was fairly stiff—which it was. But it was more than that. After twenty minutes or so I began to notice some strange things. First, I kept seeing movements of some sort out of the corners of my eyes, but whenever I turned to look there was nothing there. Then I began to see ripples rolling through the carpet. I knew it could not be so, but I kept seeing them anyway. A few minutes later the old man suddenly got up and announced:

"It's time. Come with me and I'll show you somethin' I'll bet you've never seen before."

I went with him eagerly, figuring this must be what my friend had meant by "it's worth the trip." The old man led me into another room, perhaps three by four meters in size. There was a television set in one corner. It was one of those super large screen sets, bigger than any I had ever seen. The screen was all of a meter in width and nearly as high.

"Television?" I asked.

"Not exactly," the old man replied, "it's something like TV, but different. I was going to call it Cosmavision, Univision, or something like that, but those words are just too durned long. Now I just call it The Seer."

"Seer?"

"Yep. You know, you use it to see things with, so it's a see-er."

The old man moved an armchair right in front of the big screen and told me to sit down. I protested.

"But that's too close. Everything will look blurry."

"No it won't," said the old man, "trust me!"

So I sat down in the chair. The old man began to fiddle with the controls. I noticed there were quite a few controls I could not identify. An uneasy feeling started to come over me again, but I remembered my grandfather's advice and concentrated on what was happening and not on how I was feeling about it. In a few moments a picture appeared on the screen. It was a TV show I had seen once or twice before.

"It *is* just a television set!" I exclaimed.

"Ha!" he replied. "You'll see! I'm just settin' it up now."

Sure enough, when the old man had the TV adjusted to his liking, he turned another dial and the screen went black—and I mean really black. It looked like a giant hole in the set, right in front of me. Involuntarily, I shrank back from it.

"Don't worry," the old man assured me, "it won't hurt you. You're safe enough." He chuckled again. I wondered why it was that everyone seemed to find me so amusing.

"Okay," he announced, "it's ready. Where d'you want to start?"

"Start?" I asked. "What do you mean?"

"Pick a place, any place, just so's you know it well enough that you'll recognize it when you see it. We'll start there."

I was willing to play his crazy game, so I told him to start at my grandfather's house. I waited for him to ask me where it was, but he didn't. He just looked at me very carefully and began twiddling some dials. After a while he got a satisfied look on his face, reached out, and pushed a small button near the edge of the control console. Abruptly, I could see a view of a house and yard, seen from directly above. Even from that strange angle I recognized it almost instantly: it was my grandfather's house and yard. There in the backyard was Beelzebub himself, picking fruit from a peach tree. I was dumbfounded.

"That *is* my grandfather's house! That's him, picking peaches."

"Yep," the old man agreed, looking pleased with himself.

Suddenly I had a thousand questions, but the old man brushed them aside. No time for that now, he told me, we must be getting on with it.

"Now," he continued, "which way do you want to go?"

"Which way?"

"Yep! Out or in: which'll it be? Makes no difference, you know. We can do it both ways if you like."

I hadn't a clue what he meant, but I chose going out because it sounded somehow more interesting than going in.

"Okay," he announced. "Here we go."

He punched a button with a red arrow on it pointing up; I noticed the one next to it had an arrow pointing down. Instantly the picture began to change, everything in it shrinking rapidly. Within a few seconds my grandfather's house was just a dot.

"I know what this is!" I exclaimed. "I saw something like it on television once. The picture got ten times bigger each second until you could see half the universe."

"Yep," the old man confirmed, "but this's different. For one thing, we don't have to stop anywhere 'lessen we want to. For another, those perfesser guys forgot the time factor."

"Time factor?"

"Yep! Every time you make the picture ten times bigger, you gotta speed things up ten times. Or else you lose perspective."

I saw what he meant right away. By now I could see expanses of hundreds of miles, and the clouds below were racing across the landscape as if we were watching time lapse pictures. After a couple more seconds I could see the whole world. It was spinning at a crazy rate, completing a revolution perhaps five times a second. Soon I could see the moon whirling around the earth. By the time I could see its whole orbit it was moving so fast it was just a blur.

The earth and its lunar ring (for that was what it looked like with the moon making dozens of orbits every second) continued to shrink rapidly, soon becoming tiny and hard to make out. Mars and Venus came into the picture, and then Old Sol, brilliant but incredibly small. By this time the planets, especially the inner ones, were going around the sun as fast as the moon had been orbiting the earth when last I saw it. A thrill ran through me when I realized I was seeing dozens of years go by in the space of a single second.

The old man's voice cut into my reflections.

"Here comes Jupiter," he announced. Sure enough, there it was, a small yellowish orb circling the shrinking sun like a golden bullet. By the time Saturn came into the picture it was so small and moving so fast that I couldn't make out the rings at all. In a few more seconds Uranus, Neptune, and tiny Pluto appeared in succession.

The whole solar system was now in view, about a dozen seconds having elapsed at this point. But it looked like only a very bright star with a large and very faint ring system. Even Pluto was orbiting the sun at such a rate that it was impossible to focus on. I recalled from somewhere that Pluto takes about two hundred and fifty years to make one orbit around the sun, yet here I was seeing it go around maybe fifty times a second.

"Look at the stars—haven't changed much, have they?"

Again the old man's voice broke my concentration on the fascinating show unfolding before my eyes. What he said was true, though I had been so absorbed watching the solar system that I hadn't noticed this until he pointed it out.

In the space of a few more seconds the solar system had shrunk to where it looked like a tiny whirling disc, yet the background stars had not changed appreciably in appearance.

Now, however, I saw that even the distant stars were beginning to move, slowly at first, and then more quickly. First, they began drawing closer to each other. Then they all began to move in the same direction, as though they had just been caught up in a gentle current of running water.

I watched in fascination as even more stars appeared on the screen, moving ever faster, like some immense phosphorescent waterfall, until I realized I was seeing the motion of our Milky Way galaxy itself. A second later I could see the nucleus of the galaxy, glowing with the energy of ninety million suns. A few more seconds (perhaps twenty seconds had passed since we had started) and the entire galaxy was visible, rotating so fast now that

I could not see individual stars or even star clusters. It quickly became a furiously spinning whirlpool of light.

"Beautiful, ain't she?" the old man asked, but I could make no reply. I managed only a faint nod of my head. Other galaxies were coming into view now, until the whole local group was on the screen, shrinking rapidly. Soon other clusters of galaxies came into the picture. After just a few more seconds there was only a seething mass of galactic clusters visible on the screen. Their fluid motion reminded me of a group of amoebas I had once observed under a microscope.

Suddenly the screen flashed and seemed to go blank. I was so startled I let out an involuntary yelp. The old man just laughed.

"Most folks get more spooked than that when it happens."

"What did happen?" I asked.

"We just popped out of this universe, sonny, that's all."

"What do you mean, 'that's all'? There is no other universe."

"That's what you think, sonny; I know better, and so will you pretty soon, unless you can't handle it. . . ."

The old man's voice trailed off leaving me wondering what I could expect next. Looking back, I saw the screen filled with little points of light dancing back and forth, some of them surrounded by strange glowing clouds that pulsated or whirled around them. Although these, too, rapidly shrank to insignificance, they were accreting into something vaguely familiar. I saw a rough, craggy terrain made of some translucent pink material. It quickly smoothed out into something I abruptly recognized as human skin. In less time than it takes to tell about it, this view expanded to reveal a beautiful woman lying naked on what looked to me like a sandy beach.

As her face came into view she looked directly into my eyes and smiled. I swear it was a smile of recognition. She knew me; she could see me. I felt my scalp prickling and goose bumps raising up all over my body. At that instant I realized this was getting to be even stranger than the train and its Conductor. Then the woman was gone, shrinking to a mote in a vast expanse of sandy terrain and chartreuse green ocean. Seconds later I could see the whole planet the woman lived on, which appeared to be quite a bit larger than the earth. A huge orange-red sun appeared next with a tiny brilliant blue companion; they were evidently the solar source for the woman's planet. I was still stunned by the view of the woman when the old man's voice cut through to me.

"Did you like her?" he asked, but without waiting for me to answer he went on. "I'm going to have to speed things up now or we'll never get back in one night."

So saying, the old man pushed yet another button on The Seer, twirled a dial, and suddenly the picture began expanding at a practically mind-blowing rate. In a matter of seconds whole universes sprang into view, shrank away to whirling nothingness, and were replaced by yet other universes. I sat there transfixed by what I was seeing, unable to do anything except stare in awe and wonder.

This had gone on for perhaps ten or fifteen minutes, and we had passed through literally thousands of nested universes, when the old man's voice broke the spell.

"Now watch this carefully, sonny!"

I turned my head slightly and saw the old man carefully observing some kind of counter. Abruptly he reached over and pushed another button. The screen immediately slowed down to its original pace. Once more I saw the little dancing lights that I now knew meant we were emerging into yet another universe. This time I recognized the skin before it had shrunk to anything like a normal scale. I half wondered if I was going to see yet another beautiful woman. I was not prepared for what I did see: my grandfather, still picking peaches in his backyard.

"I don't believe it!" I exclaimed.

"You'd better," replied the old man. "What you just saw was as real as anything you'll ever see, young fella."

I said nothing. I believe I was incapable of speech at that point. Seeing I was going to remain silent, the old man continued.

"Now d'you see what I meant? I *said* we could go either way!"

I nodded weakly in assent.

"There is one difference, though," he continued. "If we'd gone the other way you would've seen a man the first universe over, instead of the woman. Everything in between would've been different from what you just saw; only the ending would have been the same. We would've come down to your grandfather, instead of coming up from the inside, so to speak."

I nodded weakly again. My head was spinning. I was beginning to feel terrible. I had a splitting headache, which in my excitement I had not noticed. The old man saw how I was feeling and, acting not the least bit surprised, helped me over to a couch in an adjoining room. As soon as he had made me comfortable the old man left the room. He came back shortly with some sort of medicine, which he fed to me from a spoon. Whatever it was, it took effect quickly. In a few minutes I was asleep.

WHEN I AWOKE, sunlight was streaming in the window over the couch. I felt refreshed, with no trace of the headache I had suffered from the night before. I could, however, very well remember all that I had seen on The Seer. The old man was apparently already up, as I could hear the sounds of kitchen utensils coming from the back of the house.

I got up quietly and took the opportunity to slip into the room where The Seer was. I started to examine it more closely only to find it was just an old, dilapidated television set with ordinary TV controls. Moreover, the screen was not nearly so big as I remembered it. I concluded that the old man had spirited away The Seer during the night and replaced it with this old derelict.

Later, during breakfast with the old man, I asked him about it.

"What did you do with The Seer?"

"Nothing," he replied innocently.

"Nonsense! I was not born yesterday. You don't expect me to believe that old TV set in there is The Seer, do you?"

"Nope," came the laconic reply.

"Then where the hell is The Seer?" I demanded, becoming quite exasperated.

"You really wanna know, don't ya?" he teased. "It's right there," he said, pointing. I turned, thinking he meant behind me.

He laughed.

"Don't you see? It's you! You are The Seer. That thing in the other room is an old TV set I bought from Madman Muntz before the Korean War broke out. Still works, too."

I stared at him in disbelief. How could it be? What was happening to me? Ever since I had left my grandfather's house I had been having ever stranger experiences. Like Alice in Wonderland, I found things getting curiouser and curiouser. Nothing seemed to make sense any more.

"But I can't do things like that. I don't know how." It sounded feeble even to me, but I had to protest against this impossible charge. I was The Seer? Preposterous!

The old man looked at me kindly.

"You had some help," he said. "It was the tea. I think I gave you a bit too much."

I looked at him sharply. Those were the exact words my bearded friend had used the morning after my wild train ride. Could they be in cahoots together?

"What tea?" I asked. "What are you talking about?"

"Sorry," he replied, "I meant the curaçao."

Well, it wasn't curaçao we drank last night, I thought, but it *was* a liqueur. I decided to drop the subject. I was beginning to think I didn't really want to know any more about it.

✧   ✧   ✧

An hour or so later I took my leave. I thanked the old man for his hospitality and tried to act very pleased about the whole thing. I don't think I fooled him. As I started down the road in the warm sunshine I reflected that I had enough to mull over to keep myself busy the next few days without any effort at all.

Whose hand touches me?—my brow
—my breast—my own unasking hand—
Leading me out of self to self?

—Horace Traubel, "Illumination"

3

The Robot

The old man's home was not far behind me when I made an interesting find. Inside the pocket of my jacket was a piece of paper, which I had not put there. It was a page torn out of a diary—hand-written, I was amazed to discover, by my grandfather. This is what it said:

Oct. 23rd. Tonight I discovered a new viewpoint. I am very small, but at the same time very big. I am so tiny and insignificant that I am inside everything and everyone. I am inside you. I am even inside an ant as it scrambles its way across the sidewalk. I am like a tiny atom, even smaller than an atom, inside every created thing. Yet at the same time I hold them all within me. I enfold everything and everyone—the whole universe— within my being. I am everything and I am nothing. The mighty is humbled; the humble has become mighty. All is one and one is all. Nothing has suddenly become everything.

I thought about these words for quite some time. I realized almost at once why the old man—it must have been he—had put this page from my grandfather's diary in my pocket. It applied to my own experience as The Seer. Had I not discovered that everything in creation could be reached from either within or without? Was not this the meaning of The Seer's vision?

On the one hand, by going inside myself to smaller and smaller scales, I could uncover all existence, finally returning to my own universe. Last night, on the other hand, I went upward in scale, eventually returning to my starting place from the inside out. So it seemed as correct to say that everything was contained within me as to say that I was contained in all things—essentially what my grandfather had written in his diary. But how the old man had come by a page from my grandfather's diary was beyond me.

Yet despite having been baffled and bedeviled by my experiences, I was finally beginning to gain some understanding from them. As I walked along my self-chosen path I rehashed what had happened to me. Eventually I began to feel a connection between things I had observed from the train and what I had learned from The Seer. But I couldn't quite put my finger on what that connection was.

I was still mulling this over that evening at supper, which I had earned by doing some odd jobs for the owner of a small cafe. While eating I gradually became aware of a rather well-dressed gentleman sitting across the room. He seemed to be appraising me, as though I were a prize specimen of some sort. As I was leaving I managed to catch his eye. Instead of looking away and trying to pretend he hadn't been watching me, as most people would have done, he motioned me over to his table.

"My name is Porter—Dr. Porter," he began, waving me to sit down. "I'll come straight to the point. Would you like to be my subject in a scientific experiment?"

I was a bit taken aback by his direct approach, but his proposition did sound intriguing. I was even more interested when he told me he would pay me well for the tests I would undergo. But I wanted to know two things.

"Why me? And what does the experiment entail?"

"Naturally I would not expect you to accept the job without having heard the details first. I was going to go into that next. And why you? Let's just say I can see in you certain qualities I feel are important in a subject for this particular experiment."

"Okay, I can accept that. So what does it entail?"

"Unfortunately," he began, "I can't tell you everything, as that would completely spoil the experiment. Much of what I wish to ascertain requires what we scientists call a 'naïve subject'. That is to say, one who does not know exactly what he is being tested for. I assure you, however, there is no way this experiment can do you any harm. No way at all. It might cause some transient psychological distress, but only if you are emotionally shaky to begin with. Do you consider yourself to be a strong person?"

I laughed.

"If you knew what I've gone through the past few days without cracking up, you'd not have asked me that I assure you."

"That's exactly what I thought from observing you," replied the doctor, smiling broadly. "You'll do quite well, I'm sure."

I gave a slight start, for those were the exact words the Conductor had used the night of my train ride. Upon reflection, though, I realized they were also among the most appropriate words the doctor could have used in any event. They were quite likely coincidental. I agreed to go with him and submit to his experiment, whatever it was. We went outside and got into his car, a spanking new BMW. He drove me to his house, which was, he explained, adjacent to his laboratory. While we were en route, he asked me to tell him something about the experiences I had mentioned in the cafe. I told him about both the train and The Seer, albeit in very sketchy form, and he grew intensely interested. After I had finished he fell into thought for a few moments. Then he turned and gave me a broad grin.

"What you have just told me leads me to suspect you are a much better candidate for my experiment than I had supposed. In fact, I would venture to say you may be an ideal subject."

"Well, then," I agreed, "you have found just what you wanted, have you not?"

When we got to his house, the doctor had an assistant prepare a room for me, as it was getting quite late. Within a few minutes I was sound asleep in a very comfortable bed.

I AWOKE EARLY the next morning and joined the doctor and his assistant at breakfast. His assistant was named Gridley—I never learned his first name. He seemed a likable fellow, although I did think he was overly deferential to Dr. Porter. After eating we went directly to the laboratory. There we entered a rather large room in the middle of which was a table, rather like a surgical operating table. On the table was something that looked like a corpse. I must have looked somewhat aghast, as the doctor was quick to reassure me that all was well.

"Don't be alarmed, it isn't a dead body. It's an android, a very advanced android."

"An android?" I echoed. "You mean a robot?"

"Yes, you could call it that. We call it an android because it is intended to be as close to a human being in appearance and function as possible. It's state of the art. Your job here, in fact, is to act as the android's operator by remote control. But that is as much as I can tell you beforehand."

"That sounds intriguing, most tantalizing indeed!" I quickly took up the challenge. This promised to be even more interesting than I had imagined. "When do we start?"

"Oh, we have to run some tests on you first. You must be carefully matched to the android before we do the experiment. You understand that this *is* a scientific experiment."

And test me they did. All morning long they probed and prodded me, made recordings of my voice, tested my vision and hearing, and performed numerous other tests the nature of which I could not even guess at. When they were through with me, it was lunch time.

After a hearty meal I was led to a small room that looked like a medical doctor's examining room. Gridley, the assistant, told me I would have to wait there for about half an hour while some preparations were made. He said if I wanted to, I could lie down on the couch in the corner of the room and take a catnap. Then I was left alone with my thoughts.

I did not, however, have much time for thoughts. After only a few minutes I began to feel extraordinarily drowsy, as though I had been drugged. I lay down on the couch as I had been invited to do and within a matter of seconds fell asleep.

WHEN I AWOKE, I felt strange. As soon as I opened my eyes I knew something was wrong. Everything had a slight pink cast to it, as if seen through rose-colored glasses. Sounds, I quickly discovered, were a bit brittle and tinny. Whenever I touched something the tactile sensations were peculiar, although I would have been hard put to define in what way they were peculiar. Also, when I moved around the little room, I felt awkward and stiff. But this I easily attributed to my brief siesta on the couch, which was rather small.

I was still trying to figure out what might be wrong with me when Gridley came in and told me to follow him. He took me back to the main laboratory room. I noticed the robot was no longer lying on the table.

"Where's the ro … android?" I asked. "When do I operate it?"

"In time," answered the doctor. "We had to take the android to another lab to make some last minute adjustments to it. Meanwhile, we want to do some further tests on you. By the way, did you enjoy your nap?"

I cast a sharp glance at the doctor. I had been walking about in the little room when Gridley had come for me. How did he know I had been asleep? Then I realized one of them must have looked in on me before I woke up. How else could they have known about my little nap?

The doctor's voice cut through my ruminations.

"Please come over here," he said. "I want you to read this chart for me."

It was an ordinary eye chart. I began reading it. "P, D, C, L . . . " I broke off suddenly.

"Hey! When I first woke up, everything looked pink, but now things look normal again."

"Quick accommodation," said the doctor to his assistant. "Make a note of that."

I looked at Dr. Porter suspiciously. What did he mean by that? I decided not to ask.

In quick succession I was put through a battery of hearing and other tests, some of which I could not guess the purpose of. A few of these duplicated earlier tests I had been given, but most of them did not. I was doing a reading test when I felt a sudden twinge of pain that seemed to come from my neck near the base of my skull. At the same time, it felt somewhere else, as though it had no real connection to my body. Startled, I cried "Ouch!" and reached up toward my neck. Then, realizing that I didn't really know where the pain had come from, my eyes opened wide with surprise.

"What's the matter?" asked Dr. Porter, instantly solicitous.

"I don't know," I replied. "I felt a twinge in my neck—at least, it felt like my neck. But it seemed to come from somewhere else in a way. Not from anywhere in my body, if you know what I mean."

"Bad connection?" the doctor queried his assistant.

"Possibly," came the reply.

Dr. Porter approached me, saying, "I'm also a medical doctor." Taking my head gently in his hands he manipulated it back and forth, up and down.

"Did you feel anything?" he asked.

"No. Not a thing. Feels perfectly all right."

The doctor raised an eyebrow and looked at his assistant.

"I think the bad circuit is in there, not in here."

"Yes. I'll check it right away."

Gridley turned and was gone.

"While he's gone, is it all right if I use the rest room?" I asked, having suddenly felt an urge to urinate. The doctor looked a bit dubious but said I could.

I went into the restroom the doctor had pointed out to me. I tried to urinate two or three times, but nothing happened even though I still felt the need. It was a very frustrating experience. Finally, I gave it up as a bad job, washed my hands, and was in the act of drying them when something caught my attention. There was no mirror in the washroom—only a place with missing paint, right where a mirror would usually be above the sinks.

I walked back to the lab and asked Dr. Porter about the missing mirror. He said it had been broken accidentally and they were waiting for a new one. While he was talking I realized the urge to urinate had completely vanished, quite as though I had been successful after all. It was very peculiar. I must have looked puzzled, because the doctor asked me what my problem was. I said it was nothing, just something trivial I remembered I had not done. He accepted this, sat me down, and had me restart the interrupted reading test. In a few minutes Gridley returned.

"It was a couple of leaky diodes," he told the doctor. "I replaced them both."

The doctor nodded and turned back to the test he was running on me. But suddenly I did not want to go on. A certain suspicion had just raised its head in the back of my mind. Some of the things that had happened seemed to fit into a pattern—one I didn't like at all. I glanced furtively around the room but could see nothing that would suit the purpose I had in mind. Then I noticed a small window high up on the wall of the laboratory. It was dark. It must be evening already. Sure enough, the clock on the wall read seven. Given the season it would be dark by then. I remembered seeing a large plate glass window in the hallway leading to the laboratory. It should show a good reflection with lights inside and darkness outside. Resolving to test my theory, I got up abruptly and made a beeline for the door. Dr. Porter and Gridley were so startled they made no move to stop me until it was almost too late. Porter then tried to bar my way, but I pushed him aside. To my surprise he went sprawling on the floor, gasping for breath.

I reached the window in a few large strides. I looked into it and got the shock of my life. The face I saw looking back at me was not mine. It was the face of the android. They had turned me into a robot! My head spun. The last thing I thought was, *If the android falls down with me inside, what awful result will follow?*

When I opened my eyes, I was still standing up in front of the window. I heard Porter saying, "It's all right. He just fainted."

"All right? You make me into a robot and you have the nerve to say 'it's all right'?"

"Take it easy, relax," said the doctor in as soothing a voice as he could muster up. "You are perfectly all right, and we have *not* made you into a robot, as you put it. Come, I'll show you."

So saying, he led me down the hall and into another room. In the center of the room was a glass enclosure, and inside it was a body—mine. I was inside that glass cubicle, and yet here I was, in the robot's body, looking at myself. I couldn't believe it. I almost fainted again, but regained my poise before it was too late.

"My God! What have you done to me?" I asked.

"Nothing serious," replied Porter. "You—the you in there—are in a state of sensory deprivation. The android's sensory inputs are connected to your nervous system. When we remove the connections, you will be as good as new. I promised no physical harm would come to you, didn't I?" I made no answer, so he went on. "The twinge you felt was really you. One of the blocking diodes failed and let through a nervous impulse you should have been shielded from. Otherwise, everything went as planned. Except you figured out what was going on sooner than either of us had anticipated. Perhaps you were really too good a subject for this experiment after all."

I began to relax a little. Maybe this wasn't so bad as I had imagined. We talked about it for some minutes after that, and the two of them finally persuaded me I was in no danger. I did, however, insist they terminate the experiment and restore me to my own body immediately. They agreed to this. In turn, I agreed to let them do the switch while I was conscious.

IT WAS A FASCINATING EXPERIENCE. While I lay on the gurney they began disconnecting the android's sensory inputs and reconnecting mine. My vision went black, then suddenly came back—and I was staring up through the glass top of the sensory deprivation chamber. They reconnected the rest of my senses in the same manner. When I got up out of the glass chamber, I felt good as new, just as Dr. Porter had promised.

I went over to the table where the now lifeless robot was lying and examined it thoroughly. I noticed how accurately they had duplicated my physical features. Except for the face it looked just like me. There was even a fake scar on the right forearm, exactly where I had one from an old rock climbing accident. They said they had drugged me and made the changes while I was out cold. They told me the strange distortions I had experienced upon awakening were caused by slight inaccuracies in matching the android's sensory inputs to mine, as they had measured them in the earlier tests.

It was all quite amazing. But on reflection I saw a significant aspect to this experiment they apparently had not thought of.

"You know?" I said in a carefully measured voice, "there is one thing I believe you didn't anticipate." They both raised their eyebrows a bit. "You just showed me something I might never have discovered myself. You proved to me there is no way we can tell where we really are. We always assume that our consciousness originates in our heads. I know I always have. But when I was hooked up to the robot it was just as natural to assume that I was in the robot's head. But I wasn't there at all. I was someplace else entirely. My point is, how do we know where the true seat of our consciousness is in real life? Perhaps our real mind is in some other place." Here I made a wild guess. "Maybe it's in another dimension, some other universe. And somehow it's connected to our head, just as I was connected to the robot."

The two of them looked stunned. Suddenly Gridley began to speak, his words running together like water spilling over a falls.

"My God!" he exclaimed. "That's it!" His eyes were bugging out now, as though he were about to explode. "I've been puzzling over that for a long time. Perhaps the cerebral cortex is an antenna of some kind, and the data handling capacity is determined by its surface area. And it's used to communicate between our mind or consciousness—our awareness—and our bodies. Perhaps that explains why we can't account for all the energy the brain uses. Some of it goes into the thought waves, or whatever they are. . . . "

I believe he would have gone on, but Porter cut him short with a peremptory wave of the hand.

"Don't be ridiculous, Gridley! You're supposed to be a scientist. Don't go blithering on like that! You sound like an idiot."

"Sorry," replied Gridley meekly, but he certainly did not sound very sorry to me.

"Well, now," I remarked, "I thought his idea was intriguing. Of course, I'm not a scientist."

"No, you're not, are you?" commented the doctor, looking somewhat relieved. But I noticed Gridley smiling at me from where the doctor couldn't see him, a smile that told me we two shared a special secret.

THE REST OF MY STAY THERE was uneventful. When I left the next morning, after having been well fed and rested, we parted on good terms. And why not? They had a fairly successful experiment, and I believed that they had made a remarkable contribution to my journey of self-discovery.

And, indeed, so they had.

Caveat Emptor!

Whoever you are holding me now in hand,
Without one thing all will be useless,
I give you fair warning before you attempt me further,
I am not what you supposed, but far different.

Who is he that would become my follower?
Who would sign himself a candidate for my affections?
Are you he?

The way is suspicious, the result uncertain, perhaps destructive,
You would have to give up all else, I alone would expect to be
        your sole and exclusive standard,
Your novitiate would even then be long and exhausting,
The whole past theory of your life and all conformity to the lives
        around you would have to be abandon'd,
Therefore release me now before troubling yourself any further,
        let go your hand from my shoulders,
Put me down and depart on your way.

. . .

But these *pages* conning you con at peril,
For these *pages* and I you will not understand,
They will elude you at first and still more afterward,
       I will certainly elude you,
Even while you should think you had unquestionably caught me,
       behold!
Already you see I have escaped from you.

For it is not for what I have put into it that I have written this book,
 Nor is it by reading it you will acquire it,
Nor do those know me best who admire me and vauntingly praise me,
Nor will the candidates for my love (unless at most a very few)
       prove victorious,
Nor will my *stories* do good only, they will do just as much evil,
       perhaps more,
For all is useless without that which you may guess at many times
       and not hit, that which I hinted at;
Therefore release me and depart on your way.

  —Walt Whitman, "Whoever You Are Holding Me Now In Hand,"
     from *Leaves of Grass*, 1860, revised 1881
     (line 7 from *1860 Edition*);
     pages substituted for *leaves*; *stories,* for *poems.*

As a man is, so he sees.
As the eye is formed, such are its powers.

—William Blake,
Letter, 23 August 1799

4

The Purloined God

MY JOURNEY now took me through a hilly country with richly flowered meadows at every turn of the road. I passed only the occasional village and saw few people, so I had ample time for thinking. At last I felt I was beginning to put some of my experiences together in a coherent manner. There was, I realized at length, a common denominator running through the three things I had so far been exposed to: a change in the way I perceived reality. The train had taught me that time was not what I had supposed it to be; the Seer, that space and the universe were not what I had imagined them to be; and the robot, that even I was not what I had thought myself to be. I was being gradually introduced to a radically new view of the world, and it was demolishing most of my old concepts about the way things are.

What, I began to wonder, would be my next mind-blowing experience? And how had my grandfather managed to orchestrate this path of learning for me? For by now I was convinced that Beelzebub was behind all of this. There were just too many coincidences for me to accept. I recalled an old military adage: once is a random event, twice is coincidence, three times is enemy action. Well, I had enemy action all right, but thankfully it was a friendly enemy I faced. Yet even then I suspected I never would solve this mystery.

The answer to my first question was not long in coming. As usual, it came in a way I did not anticipate. I was resting in the shade of a large cottonwood tree near a sleepy mountain hamlet when I was approached by a young man about my own age.

"Hello," he said. "Mind if I join you?"

I didn't mind, and as he sat beside me I looked him over casually. He was about my height and build, but his face was narrower than mine and his hair was very light, almost white where the sun had bleached it. His eyes were remarkable: they were the deepest, most piercing blue eyes I think I have ever seen. I liked him immediately.

"Well!" he remarked. "You look as though you've been out in the weather just about as long as I have. Are you going somewhere or just wandering?"

"Neither," I replied. It was my turn to have some fun. "I don't know where I'm going, but I'm getting there anyway."

"All right!" To my surprise he seemed pleased by what I had tried to make into a very mysterious pronouncement. I quickly found out why: he was on almost exactly the same mission as I was. The circumstances, of course, were different and not of any particular relevance to my story. But we were both searching for our selves and the meaning of life, so to speak, and thus would soon become good friends.

While we rested together under the cottonwood tree I told my newfound friend about my strange experiences of the past few days. He told me his name: Vadid—which he pronounced *Vah-deed*—and, as I reflected later, not much else. I had the feeling that he had journeyed much longer than I and did not wish to display his greater knowledge, for fear that he might seem to be boasting or lording it over me. At length he brought out of his knapsack a tattered, well-worn book titled *The Purloined God.*

"Take this," he said. "It has served me well, but I know it from cover to cover now, almost as well as I know my own face. It is time to pass it on, and I perceive that it will do you good service, just as it did me. Don't be deceived by the title; the guy who wrote it isn't a Jesus-freak or anything so simple-minded as that. The main thing he says is that the priesthood has stolen God away from us and hidden Him where no one would expect to find Him—right out in plain sight, just like the purloined letter. By leading us to believe God is some hoary old guy up in heaven, they've hidden Him from us. Because He is really everywhere, in everything and everyone. But the book is much heavier than its theme suggests. I can't even begin to tell you how heavy it really is. You'll just have to read it and see for yourself. If you can accept what he says, you'll learn plenty, I can assure you."

He said this in such a confident tone of voice that I knew he was right. I told him I would return the book to him when I had finished reading it, but he wouldn't hear of it.

"No!" he said firmly. "I'm done with it. Now it's yours. It's your turn. When you're done with it, you'll come across someone who needs it more than you do, just as I came across you. I want you to give it to that person, whomever it may be. That is my intention and my wish."

"Then," I affirmed, "so be it."

And we started out together, friends already.

LATER THAT DAY we were resting after having worked for our suppers. I was leafing through *The Purloined God,* skimming here and there as it is my habit to do with a new book. I came across this passage, which I found pertinent to what I had gone through in the past few days:

Remember that you can never experience anything other than yourself. Your entire world is part of you, a part of your personal experience. You carry it with you wherever you go. Whatever there may be that is outside your self, you can never know any of it. You can never know anyone but yourself. All of time, all of space, and all things are seen and measured by you in relationship to your self, your own personal universe. Einstein said that all measurements are relative to the frame of reference of the observer. He didn't go quite far enough. *Everything* is relative to the observer, including his so-called frame of reference, which he carries inside himself.

I was intrigued by these statements. They seemed to speak to me personally.

"Vadid," I said. "Listen to this." I read him the passage. "What is he really saying? Am I not truly experiencing you at this very minute? I mean, you're not a part of me. I see you outside me."

"No," he replied, "you do not see me. You see the part of yourself you call 'Vadid,' and which you call into being whenever you believe you see me."

"Oh, I see." I said, but I didn't really—not then, anyway.

I kept mulling these things over in my mind, trying to understand what I was being presented with. After a bit I suddenly recalled an incident from long ago, one which had always puzzled me. My cousin, who is a year or so younger than I, was visiting us. He came down with a raging fever one day, and a doctor was summoned. He gave the boy an injection of some sort and several different pills. One of the pills apparently caused my cousin to become delirious. He suddenly jumped out of bed and tried to get out of the house, saying repeatedly, "I've got to get out of here." It took three of us to restrain him, and in the process one of us was hurt by his flailing arms. All during this commotion I had the peculiar sensation that I was the one who was freaking out, not my cousin. I began to see some sort of connection between that and what I had read in *The Purloined God*.

"Vadid," I began. "Let me tell you about something strange that happened to me once." I told him the story about my cousin's delirium and my feeling that it was really happening to me instead of to him. When I had finished, Vadid smiled.

"Don't you see?" he asked. "You were right. It really was you freaking out, not him. Do you see why?"

Suddenly I was convinced I did, indeed, know why.

"Yes. I believe I understand. It was part of me that was freaking out, the part of me I call my cousin, just as you said. Later, my cousin told me he had what he thought at the time was a perfectly good reason for trying to get out of the house. He didn't feel he was freaking out at all. That always puzzled me. But now I can see it was part of my own mind, my own consciousness, the part I call my cousin, that was going nuts. A part of my own mind was displaying what I judged to be psychotic behavior, and it upset the hell out of me. Now I can finally see why."

"Great!" Vadid replied. "You're getting it. You are not so far from the ways of knowledge as you perhaps believed, are you?"

I had to agree. Five days ago all the concepts I had been using in this discussion would have been utterly alien to me. Now, they were fast becoming second nature. Was this, I began to wonder, what was referred to as a rebirth? A small shiver ran up my back at this thought. But I was getting somewhere. My grandfather hadn't sent me on a fool's errand after all.

Lying awake that night under the stars, I pondered where I was and where I was going. I had many things to sort out. This new principle that all experience was intensely personal required me to rethink literally hundreds of allied concepts. All these years I had not only believed there was an objective world to which I was exposed and to which I responded but that I also experienced this world. I saw this world, heard it, felt it, tasted it, touched it—or so I had believed. Now I found that all I had ever experienced was myself.

"Vadid," I asked softly, "are you still awake?"

"Yes."

"Tell me. I don't quite understand this yet. I see a thing, yet I do not really see it. What is it then? If we both see the same thing, and we agree as to what it is, are we not seeing the thing itself?"

"No. We are each seeing a picture that we ourselves have put together from some external stimulus. We agree on what it is only because of cultural conditioning. For instance, assume we are looking at a rose. We agree that it is a red rose because once a long time ago some adult told us that such a thing is a rose and is colored red. Even if it looks entirely different to the two of us, we shall still agree about this. We have, in effect, agreed to agree, if you see what I mean. Agreeing on an external fact proves only that the stimulus for it came from some common source, not that the world as such exists. We can never know anything more about the outside world (whatever that means) than that under certain circumstances we get common stimuli from it. This tells us nothing about the true nature of this hypothetical outside world. In other words, the world is an illusion. It could be a gigantic hoax. Perhaps there is no world, but God creates all the correct stimuli at just the right times to convince us there is such a world. How could we ever know, one way or the other?"

I had no answer to this. But I saw what he meant. I now had a feel for this new idea. I could grab it and hold onto it long enough to examine it. It was becoming real for me. I thought about it for a long time before falling to sleep.

In the morning I thought of more questions.

"Vadid," I began as we were preparing to break camp. "What about the internal pictures we make of things. How are they like mere images and not real, as we believe them to be?"

"Well," he replied, "let me ask you a question that will make it clearer to you. When you play a recording of some music, is it the original sounds you hear or only a copy?"

"A copy, of course. My grandfather told me that Buddha once said 'There is no heaped up music' or something like that." (For just an instant my grandfather's words echoed in my mind: "It will come back to you when you need to know. Then you will understand.")

"Precisely. Now, consider this: When you see something like an image of me, you are seeing it, so to speak, with your mind's eye. The image you see with your mind's eye has been constructed by your subconscious mind, if you will. It makes this image out of certain electrochemical impulses it received from the optic nerves running from your eyes to your brain. This is how music is created from a recording. Wiggles along the groove of a record, for instance, are first changed into electrical signals. These signals are amplified and fed into a loudspeaker, which changes them back into sound waves that your ears pick up. Your ears change these vibrations back into electrochemical signals. Those signals are transmitted to your brain and changed back into something—we don't really know what—that your mind's ear experiences as sound."

"In other words," I broke in, "what we see and hear are really just images of the real thing. But aren't they rather accurate? I mean, we can agree we are hearing, say, a Mozart sonata, or the Beatles, and that we are both seeing a quarter-phase moon rising over that hill."

"True, but that's not enough to prove accuracy, by any means. In the first place, all human beings could be seeing the same kind of terribly distorted images of things. But none of us would ever know, because we should all agree on what we see. In the second place, even if our separate images are personally distorted, we can't know that either. All those images were once identified for us by someone else as being what we were observing at the time. Therefore, we shall always see such an object—if I may use the term—as just what it has always been for us. And in the third place, we need not look far to find a likely source of personal distortions. Our own subconscious processes act on every image, of whatever nature, perceived by our conscious minds. And I'm sure I need not elaborate on the various kinds of psychological distortions that have been observed to occur in certain persons. After all, several branches of psychiatry are based on just such distortions. How often have you seen things you found out later weren't there, or weren't as they appeared to be?"

"Quite often, I'm sure," I replied. "I'm beginning to see what you mean."

I thought about it for a few moments and continued.

"You know, I just now thought of something that happened to me several years ago. I have an older sister, and she and I don't get along very well. My mental image of her is that of a rather dour individual. Then one day I was standing on the sidewalk when I observed a very attractive young woman walking down the sidewalk towards me. I watched her for a minute or two, thinking to myself, *Now that's the kind of woman I'd like to meet.* Then, as she approached more closely, I suddenly recognized her as my sister. Snap! Her face instantly distorted into the usual dour image that I had of her. It was as though her face had been stretched like a rubber mask into that of a beautiful woman, only to snap back into place the instant I recognized her. For the first time I realized my image of her might not correspond to the way others saw her."

"Exactly what I was saying!" agreed Vadid. "So long as you did not recognize your sister, you formed a more general image of her face. But the instant you recognized her, your internal filter went to work and produced the image you were used to seeing. That is precisely why I say you don't perceive the world directly, but only your own internal image of it.

"So far, so good. At least you know you're getting somewhere. It will make the rest of your journey that much easier for you. Trust me, you've got a long way to go, just as I have, and you will need all the help you can get."

"Okay," I agreed, a bit impatiently, "Hurray for me! But these images we see and hear: how is it they seem to us to be the real thing and not just a reproduction?"

"Ah! That's the mystery of it all. Remember, you create your own universe within your consciousness. That universe is a replica of the one you believe your senses are telling you is there. That we are perceiving the outside world, of course, we all take on faith, so to speak, without really knowing we are doing so."

"I see. This means that within my personal universe I am the Creator, does it not?"

"It certainly does! You are the Creator of the only universe, the only world, you will ever know in this life."

"Man, that's really heavy!" I replied. "That must be what the Bible means when it says we are made in the image of God. He creates the universe, and we create our own mini-universe within us. Wow! It means I am like God, within myself anyway."

"Yes," said Vadid, grinning hugely, "and you are God in more ways than that, my friend."

I wanted Vadid to tell me more about how I was "God in more ways than that," but he would not. He said to try to explain it to me then would only confuse me, saying I should wait for the proper time, when all things necessary would be revealed to me. I pressed him a bit, but he was so clearly adamant in his position that I soon gave up. As I discovered later, he was almost certainly right. I wasn't ready for it.

LATER THAT SAME DAY I got something I wasn't ready for anyway, whether I wanted it or not. Vadid and I were passing through a town of modest size when we witnessed a brawl between a man and a teenaged girl we assumed to be his daughter. There was much shouting and yelling, and the man began beating on the poor girl with a stick. Before we could even think of doing anything about it, someone else, apparently a neighbor, intervened. As we walked away, Vadid seemed lost in thought. He finally looked up and made a comment about what we had seen.

"Poor guy," he said, shaking his head.

"Guy?" I retorted. "That was no guy. It was a girl."

"I wasn't talking about the girl," he countered. "Why should I feel sorry for her? She'll soon get over it; the man never will, not completely anyway."

"Get over what?" I asked. "A guilty conscience?"

"No," Vadid laughed as he spoke, "the bad karma."

"I don't know about your 'bad karma'," I said deliberately, "but I think I'd rather take my chances with it than have the bruises from that stick all over my back."

"That's because you don't understand the way the world works. You're describing things the way most people see them. That does not mean you're right. When you get to a better place, you'll see that things are much different than they appear to be."

"Oh!" I exclaimed, beginning to see a connection. "Is that what it meant in *The Purloined God* where it said that the external world is only an illusion?"

"Yes," came the reply. "But be careful. The world is an illusion only in the way it works, not in its basic reality. To confuse those two is a fundamental error. One, I might add, that is very common for Westerners to make when they study Eastern traditions."

"How does it work, then?"

"Well, basically it's all part of the same scene we were talking about yesterday. Remember, the universe you experience is your own private universe and no one else's. You are here for only one reason: to learn. The results of your learning, whether they prove to be good or bad (as we know good and bad), apply to you alone and to no one else. I agree that your actions may appear to affect others: that is precisely the illusion the author of *The Purloined God* is talking about. The truth is that your own actions, whether for good or for evil, affect only you no matter how much it may appear to be otherwise. So, I said I was sorry for the man, not for the girl. For her, the reality of the bruises is only apparent and very temporary. Eventually she will see they were like bruises received in a dream. And just as surely, the man will someday discover that his actions hurt only himself and not the girl. Nasty blow, eh?"

"Pardon the pun," he added as a sort of afterthought.

"Well, I guess so," I agreed hesitantly. "But I'm afraid I'm going to have to mull this over for a while before I can come to terms with it. It's a whole lot to swallow in one sitting, if you know what I mean."

"Oh, I hear you, okay? I know exactly where you're coming from. I've been there myself, and not very long ago, either."

"Come on, Vadid, you're so far beyond me it's pathetic!"

"No," Vadid replied firmly. "I'm not beyond you or above you; I'm just in a different place, that's all. This path we're both on does not come in incremental stages, higher and higher, or farther and farther; it's just a succession of different places."

This was quite enough for me to chew on for one afternoon, so I quit talking and began doing some serious thinking. We walked on in silence. I was beginning to see the light at the end of the tunnel, or so I thought at the time. In reality I was just seeing a little way around the next bend in the path. I had a long way to go, and there would be many major jolts along the way. My consciousness was just beginning to open up.

To You

Whoever you are, I fear you are walking the walks of dreams,
I fear these supposed realities are to melt from under your feet
      and hands,
Even now your features, joys, speech, house, trade, manners,
      troubles, follies, costume, crimes, dissipate away from you,
Your true soul and body appear before me,
They stand forth out of affairs, out of commerce, shops, work, farms,
      clothes, the house, buying, selling, eating, drinking,
      suffering, dying.

Whoever you are, now I place my hand upon you, that you be my
      poem,
I whisper with my lips close to your ear,
I have loved many women and men, but I love none better than you.
Oh I have been dilatory and dumb,
I should have made my way straight to you long ago,
I should have blabb'd nothing but you, I should have chanted
      nothing but you.

I will leave all and come and make the hymns of you,
None has understood you, but I understand you,
None has done justice to you, you have not done justice to yourself,
None but has found you imperfect, I only find no imperfection in you,
None but would subordinate you, I only am he who will never consent
      to subordinate you,
I only am he who places over you no master, owner, better, God,
      beyond what waits intrinsically in yourself.

Painters have painted their swarming groups and the centre-figure
    of all,
From the head of the centre-figure spreading a nimbus of gold-color'd
    light,
But I paint myriads of heads, but paint no head without its
    nimbus of gold-color'd light,
From my hand from the brain of every man and woman it streams,
    effulgently flowing forever.

Oh I could sing such grandeurs and glories about you!
You have not known what you are, you have slumber'd upon yourself
    all your life,
Your eyelids have been the same as closed most of the time,
What you have done returns already in mockeries,
(Your thrift, knowledge, prayers, if they do not return in mockeries,
    what is their return?)

The mockeries are not you,
Underneath them and within them I see you lurk,
I pursue you where none else has pursued you,
Silence, the desk, the flippant expression, the night,
        the accustom'd routine,
        if these conceal you from others or yourself,
        they do not conceal you from me,
The shaved face, the unsteady eye, the impure complexion,
        if these balk others they do not balk me,
The pert apparel, the deform'd attitude, drunkenness, greed,
        premature death, all these I part aside.
There is no endowment in man or woman that is not tallied in you,
There is no virtue, no beauty in man or woman, but as good is in you,
No pluck, no endurance in others, but as good is in you,
No pleasure waiting for others, but an equal pleasure waits for you.

As for me, I give nothing to anyone except I give the like carefully
    to you,
I sing the songs of the glory of none, not God, sooner than I sing the
    songs of the glory of you.

Whoever you are! claim your own at any hazard!
These shows of the East and West are tame compared to you,
These immense meadows, these interminable rivers,
    you are immense and interminable as they,
These furies, elements, storms, motions of Nature,
    throes of apparent dissolution,
    you are he or she who is master or mistress over them,
Master or mistress in your own right over Nature, elements, pain,
    passion, dissolution.

The hopples fall from your ankles, you find an unfailing sufficiency,
Old or young, male or female, rude, low, rejected by the rest,
    whatever you are promulges itself,
Through birth, life, death, burial, the means are provided,
    nothing is scanted,
Through angers, losses, ambition, ignorance, ennui, what you are
    picks its way.

        —Walt Whitman,
           from *Leaves of Grass*
           1856 edition

All the world's a stage,
And all the men and women merely players.
They have their exits and their entrances,
And one man in his time plays many parts.

—Shakespeare,
As You Like It, Act 1, Scene 1

5

Vadid's Folly

he next day Vadid and I left the mountainous country we had been passing through and entered a more desert landscape. It was hilly and much more barren than anything I had seen since leaving my grandfather's house nine or ten days ago. Before we had walked far through this new land we got into some more serious conversations. The first one began when I asked Vadid why the world seemed to be designed in such a peculiar fashion.

"Why is it," I began, "that the world is made in such a way as to deceive us almost completely as to its true nature?"

"You do ask some heavy questions!" replied Vadid, laughing gently. "But the answer is deceptively simple: it wouldn't work any other way."

"What do you mean by that?"

"That's the heavy part. For starters, how many people do you know who wouldn't run amok if they knew they could do no real harm in the world?"

"Damn few!" It was my turn to laugh.

"Yes, I agree. It might be helpful for you to think of the world as a sort of lifetime test. A test you can't really fail, and one you certainly can't ace. At least, no more than two or three in the history of the world ever have, if even they have. What's more, this test only works if those taking it don't know they are taking a test until they are almost finished with it. And that can happen when they are only your age, or when they are quite old. In many cases, it won't happen in an entire lifetime."

"Why is that? The last part, I mean?"

"I'm afraid I can't really explain it to you now. First, you probably wouldn't understand the answer. And second, if I told you and you didn't understand, it might well impede your progress. And that's the last thing either of us wants, right?"

I had to agree, but just the same it didn't help much. I still felt a gnawing desire to know more. I tried another tack.

"Well then, why is the world made in such a way that we can't do any real harm to anyone but ourselves?"

"Would you," he rejoined, "turn loose a gang of kindergarten kids with loaded machine guns to play with?"

"No, certainly not!"

"Nor would I. On a more adult level, would you let a person who was studying to become an engineer design real bridges that people were going to use?"

Before I could reply to the question he answered it himself.

"No, again, right? That's why we have schools where people can learn how to do things and their mistakes won't cause disasters. Their mistakes affect only themselves. Well, that's exactly the way life is designed. We do make mistakes, many of them. Yet they hurt no one but us. The world, you see, is a gigantic classroom where people are learning how to live."

"Wow!" I exclaimed, "I never thought of it that way before."

"Well, then," Vadid rejoined, "it's high time you did, isn't it? There's no time like the present—it's the only time there is."

I quickly agreed with that. If there was one thing I had learned from my experiences thus far, it was that the Conductor was right: It's always *now*.

I THOUGHT IN SILENCE for quite a while about how the world could be a classroom for us to learn how to live. The more I thought about it the more sense it made. It gave me both a thrill of accomplishment that I had learned something important and a sense of the supernatural. Here, right in my own head, was solid evidence that there was a real purpose to the universe. We are not a cosmic freak show, an accidental product of blind, unthinking natural forces. Neither are we a mere curiosity produced from a singular throw of some cosmic dice. We are not a vagary of nature; we are here for a reason. The new sense of purpose this viewpoint brought into my awareness made my whole improbable pilgrimage seem worthwhile for perhaps the first time.

I had always wondered about this. On the one hand, I can't accept the milksop teachings of organized religions. They make no sense to me. More than that, they are so fantastic as to stretch my credulity to the breaking point. On the other hand, however, I could never bring myself to believe that the universe and we humans are the product of unthinking forces. We're not just the chance effect of some random cause. There must be more to it than that. Otherwise, life is drained of all meaning, and the so-called verdict of history is but a fool's judgment. After all, the universe will eventually grind to a halt, either by shrinking back into the cosmic egg from which it sprang or by dying a slow entropic death. In the first case it ends with a reverse bang; in the second, with less than a whimper. Certainly the time will come when no one will be left to give a hot damn about anything. Then what difference will it make how I or anyone else had once behaved? Such a view of things drains life of all moral significance. I need more than that. We all do. Now I saw there is an answer, if only we have eyes to see and ears to hear.

VADID'S VOICE interrupted my thoughts.

"I'm going to stop here for a bit," he said.

I found we were standing in the road in front of a small cottage set well back from the road. It was surrounded by desert landscaping. I watched Vadid walk around the house and disappear behind it. Perhaps five minutes later he reappeared in the company of a delightful young woman. She looked about my own age and attractive. She had light brown hair that fell to her shoulders, a few freckles, and the prettiest doe-like eyes I had ever seen. She was wearing cut-off shorts made from old, faded blue jeans, and a thin white blouse. Vadid introduced her to me as Running Deer, obviously an Indian name, although it was just as obvious that she was no Indian. After a bit of chit-chat, Vadid and Running Deer excused themselves and left me to my ruminations. It wasn't difficult to guess what they were up to. I did think it strange, however, for someone as seemingly spiritual as Vadid to indulge in casual relations with a woman he saw only occasionally. As I was to find out somewhat later, however, this encounter was anything but casual .

✧   ✧   ✧

AN HOUR OR SO LATER Vadid and Running Deer reappeared and invited me to join them for lunch. I did so gladly.

Our lunch together proved uneventful, and Vadid and I were soon on our way again. I thought several times of asking him for some explanation of what I considered to be his somewhat deviant conduct with Running Deer. But each time I thought better of it.

We settled down for the evening in a picturesque little canyon strewn with yuccas and agaves. Vadid pulled out a small paper bag from his knapsack and emptied its contents onto a sheet of paper on the ground in front of him. It looked to me like a pile of cucumber slices that had dried up and curled a bit at the edges. I asked him what it was.

"Peyote," he answered. "Running Deer gave it to me just before we left."

"Hey!" I said. "Isn't that stuff dangerous?"

"You bet it is! If you don't know how to use it. Almost anything is dangerous—in the hands of an ignorant person."

As it turned out, he wanted me to join him in eating some of the peyote. I was very reluctant to do that, but he assured me repeatedly that it would do me no harm. So I gave in and agreed to join him. It was without a doubt the bitterest, most nauseating stuff I have ever eaten. It took me a good half an hour to eat the pieces Vadid had given me, which I noticed comprised rather less than half the total. Vadid ate the rest himself.

Forty minutes or so passed and I had yet to notice any effects from the peyote I had eaten. I complained about this to Vadid, but he just smiled in a strange, knowing manner.

"Well," I said, "at least nothing bad is happening to me. I see you were right about that, anyway."

He just smiled again and said nothing. I had not long to wonder why he smiled so. About ten minutes later I began to go through some changes. First, I realized everything looked different in a subtle, numinous way. Then I began seeing colors in everything I looked at, colors that hadn't been there just a few minutes ago—and this despite the growing darkness.

"Vadid," I said softly, "this stuff is fantastic. I feel freer than I ever have before. Is this all there is to it?"

Vadid only smiled again.

That wasn't all there was to it. Before much longer I felt my whole personality beginning to dissolve, as it were. I think this would have frightened me had it not been for the strange experiences I had already been through in the past week. As it was, I was able to relax and enjoy what I was experiencing.

I looked at Vadid, thinking to ask him another question. I stopped short, however, as he looked much different than he had a few minutes before (or was it a few hours before?). He looked like a clown, a joker. I had to laugh. It was just too much. I laughed hard for several minutes, until Vadid finally looked up and stared straight into my eyes.

"This is merely my controlled folly," he said solemnly.

"Your what?" His answer sent me into more peals of laughter. After enduring some minutes of my laughing, he turned to me and spoke. And again his solemn voice made an absurd contrast with his comic appearance. It was like the voice of God coming from a court jester.

"Yes," he pronounced, "you are near the transparent stage."

This time I just stared at him. Ideas about what he meant by those words churned through my mind like a flash flood. In a few more minutes (or hours?) I saw what he was talking about. His skin had turned into what looked like fine, translucent white china. And underneath his skin I could see something else, something not like his face at all. This vision slowly solidified until I could see it was my own face, seen dimly as if in a clouded mirror. What a shock! I got up and walked away, not wanting to sit where I could see my face underneath his. Feeling a bit giddy, I reached out for the branch of a small river willow. As soon as I touched it I felt the touch myself, as if someone had grabbed hold of my arm. I pulled back my hand, reached out and touched the branch again. The same thing happened. This time I held on to it. I soon noticed something else even stranger. I could feel the breeze blowing through me, precisely as though I were made out of branches and leaves myself. When I touched the branch, I felt the breeze go through me; when I pulled away, I no longer felt it. Suddenly I realized what I had been seeing and feeling. It was only myself. Had I not just learned that everything I experienced was a part of me? Why then should I be disturbed when I experienced it more directly under the peculiar state of consciousness induced in me by the peyote? I resolved not to let it bother me any more, and it did not.

Before that night was over I had clearly seen the illusory nature of both the world and my own self. Never again would I be so naïve as I had been before starting my pilgrimage.

I also experienced something else, something I could never quite put into words. I discovered another reality to the world, one that transcends ordinary experience in a decisive way. While I was in the altered state of consciousness brought on by the peyote (and this was almost the only effect it had on me) I could feel and sense this in much the same way that I know when I am awake and not dreaming. I couldn't put my finger on it, but nonetheless I knew it was there with absolute certainty. Afterwards, I could remember having this experience and how it affected me, but I could no longer remember the experience itself. I could no longer capture it, so to speak. I found this very frustrating at the time.

I was rather surprised that I experienced none of the bizarre effects that Carlos Castaneda reported in *The Teachings of Don Juan*. I still wonder about it from time to time. Yet I cannot say I was disappointed with what did happen. For a few short hours I looked straight into the heart of the universe and saw myself for the first time. I liked what I saw. Later I would find this odd, but at the time it seemed axiomatic.

We woke up late the next afternoon. I plied Vadid with questions about my peyote experience. I got precious little in the way of answers. Except just once, when I asked him about Mescalito.

"I didn't see Mescalito," I said matter-of-factly.

"No," he said, as though he already knew that. "Perhaps Mescalito did not want you to see him. Or it may be that you did not eat enough peyote to see him."

"Does the peyote produce Mescalito?"

"No, peyote produces nothing. It only enables you to see whatever it is you do see. Peyote opens the gate, but it is up to you to go through and find out what is on the other side."

I thought about my experience with the willow tree. It seemed to confirm what Vadid was saying. I shook my head in unspoken affirmation. Then I changed the subject.

"Vadid, what is Running Deer to you?"

He stood silently for a few moments, as if weighing whether he should answer my question. Finally he said quietly, "A friend. A very good friend."

"I'll say!" I quickly grabbed the opening he had given me. "But tell me: How can you carry on such a casual relationship with a woman you see only once in a while?"

As soon as the words left my mouth I was sorry. Yet to my surprise, instead of showing irritation Vadid only smiled.

"We complete each other," he said. "When we're together, we are one. And when we're not together, we are never really apart."

It was an interesting reply, but I didn't understand it. I could not comment on what he had said intelligently, so I just changed the direction of our conversation.

"That's something I couldn't do," I said. "I could never carry on an occasional physical relationship with a woman."

"You have a lot to learn about sexuality," he observed, a secret little smile playing about the corners of his mouth.

"Perhaps," I conceded, "but I do know what I like and what I don't like."

"Do you?" His tone of voice told me that he wondered whether I really knew what I was talking about.

I began to wonder myself. Since last night—in fact, since beginning my journey of self-discovery—I kept finding I was not so sure about many things I had formerly felt quite positive about. Now I realized that this subject might fit into that category as well. I fell silent, lost in my thoughts.

We walked together for several hours, not talking much, until at length we came to a fork in the road. For some reason I could not fathom, one of the roads seemed to beckon to me. I tried to ignore it, but could not. This road, which I had never seen before, held a strange fascination for me. I just had to see where it went. Vadid, it turned out, was going the other way. Reluctantly, we parted company.

I was on my own again.

✧   ✧   ✧

THAT EVENING, as I relaxed in my makeshift camp, I resumed browsing through The Purloined God. One section struck me right between the eyes, so pertinent was it to the subject Vadid and I had been discussing earlier in the day.

> God Itself can only be approached through a synthesis, a synthesis that is partly sexual in nature. One must know his or her own bisexuality before knowing God. It must be clearly perceived that male and female are like the inside and the outside of a cup . . . or the inside and outside of God. Male and female are God passing Itself in two directions at once . . . at One. We meet here in the middle, immersed in Love—if only we can see it.
>
> > Together, we make God as we make love.
> > Separately, there are the two of us,
> > Still God Together, but all unknowing . . .
> > Male without female desires completion;
> > Female without male desires completion;
> > Together we become perfected, completed . . .
> > Consummated . . . .
>
> Only thus merged is there perfection—the complementing of each other, for each other, through each other, and in God. As One, we are two; as two, we are One alone. . . .

Out of habit formed in the past several days, I turned to ask Vadid for a comment on this passage. He was not there. I had a sudden sense of loss, and yet something within me would not admit this loss. Something told me that wherever I went Vadid would be with me in some way I could not yet understand.

Still, I felt very much alone just then. I also began to sense a certain foreboding, a premonition of something really heavy going down. I wanted help in meeting this new challenge, yet I knew it could not be.

What I would face, I knew I must face alone.

Man, was I ever wrong!

Unfolded only out of the folds of the woman
  man comes unfolded, and is always
  to come unfolded ...
Unfolded only out of the inimitable poems of woman
  can come the poems of man,
  (Only thence have my poems come) ...

—Walt Whitman, "Poem of Women"
from *Leaves of Grass*, 1856 Edition

6

Lilith

The next morning I awoke refreshed and invigorated. I could remember having had a sense of foreboding the night before, but I no longer felt that way. I had no idea why this should have been so, and I wasted no more time thinking about it. I went on my way, though I knew not whence, in higher spirits than I could recall having enjoyed since beginning my pilgrimage. Was it only two weeks ago I had left? It felt like years ago. The radical changes I had gone through seemed to have stretched time.

Before going very far that day I noticed a distinct change in the countryside. The desert was gradually giving way to a hillier terrain with more vegetation. Soon trees and then forests began to appear along the higher ridges. In the distance I caught glimpses of rocky peaks streaked with summer snow fields.

I stopped in a fair-sized mountain village for lunch. By then I had become totally reliant upon Beelzebub's advice and no longer questioned the strange ways in which my livelihood seemed to fall into my lap. While eating I was startled to hear a vaguely familiar female voice calling my name. It was Running Deer. Her hair was braided now down both sides of her head. She was wearing a long black dress adorned only by a simple pendant consisting of an uncut turquoise nugget and two bear claws on a silver chain. The effect of all this was to make her look much more like an Indian than she had the first time I saw her.

"Running Deer! What are you doing here?" I asked.

"I have a message for you. Your grandfather wants you to go to Beaver Valley. It's over that ridge." She pointed over my shoulder.

"My grandfather! How do you know my grandfather?"

She looked me straight in the eye.

"I don't," she said evenly. "I've never even met him."

"Then how . . ." I began but quickly stopped. I could see by the look in her eyes it would be useless to push further. By this time I had learned there were some things it did not pay to question. I was also getting used to the unexpected, so it no longer bothered me when weird things happened.

"Okay," I gave up. "Why am I supposed to go there?"

"I don't know," she replied, flashing a beautiful smile. "You are just supposed to go."

I realized I already knew all I was going to find out about this new direction, at least until I got there, so I agreed to go. Running Deer appeared disinterested in my response, which for some reason did not surprise me a bit. In a few minutes I was on my way, wondering what I was getting myself into this time. I considered the train and its strange conductor, The Seer, the robot, and my adventures with Vadid. I tried to find a pattern to indicate the next direction my pilgrimage would take. It was hopeless, I know, but at the time it seemed a worthwhile endeavor. At any rate, it did keep me occupied on a rather long and grueling hike up and over the ridge Running Deer had pointed out to me (she had told me it was about twenty-five miles out of the way to go around the ridge, so I had chosen the direct route).

By the time I got to the summit of the ridge, the weather, which had started out gloriously clear, had deteriorated into a flat gray overcast. As I began descending to the valley floor a drizzle began, so fine it was almost a mist. It kept up all the way to the bottom.

When I finally reached a creek running along the valley floor, I was not in a good mood. I must have let the gloomy weather get the better of me. In any event, I felt as blank and featureless as the sky. I had no idea what I was supposed to do there, if anything, or what was supposed to happen. I began wandering aimlessly, finally picking my way through the forest along the creek watching the occasional beavers for amusement.

AFTER HALF AN HOUR of wandering about in this manner I came to a beautiful clearing in the woods. It was covered with lush grass and multi-colored wild flowers. I sat down on a rock at the edge of the clearing, as I had nothing better to do. I could hear the brook nearby. Its happy gurgling clashed sharply with my dismal gray mood. I noticed it was getting quite dark considering there should have been at least two hours of daylight left. Then I heard the reason: a low rumbling of thunder that echoed and re-echoed off the valley walls. I began looking about for a likely place to find shelter and caught sight of something moving.

At first I saw only a pale ghost drifting through the mist in the trees beyond the clearing. It looked so eerie that I shuddered and the back of my neck prickled. Then my ghost was into the clearing and I could see it was a woman with a fantastic body. And she was stark naked.

I sat there, frozen to the rock. What was she doing here? Why was she wandering around naked on this chilly, clammy afternoon? Who was she? Was I dreaming? Questions raced through my mind in a flash. For a moment I thought perhaps she didn't see me sitting there, but as she drew closer I could see she was looking right at me. She smiled, an amused but friendly smile. She seemed to be enjoying the effect she no doubt knew she was having on me. She didn't seem the least bit embarrassed by her nakedness. I was though—I could feel the blood rushing to my face.

For a brief instant I considered running away but made no move. I felt hypnotized by this female apparition that was steadily closing in on me. By this time I could see her plainly. She had gray hair, yet she was not old. Her body was young, slender, and nubile: flat tummy with a shallow navel, breasts fairly full but so firm they barely jiggled as she walked. Her eyebrows were very dark but her pubic hair was the same soft gray as the hair that swirled around her shoulders and cascaded past her breasts almost to her hips. As I stared in wonder I realized my eyes were right at the level of her crotch. So I stood up slowly, half expecting her to take off abruptly like a startled deer. Instead she spoke.

"Hello!" she said warmly, apparently totally unabashed.

"Well, hello!" I tried to sound nonchalant but my voice croaked horribly. My mouth felt stuffed full of cotton. She laughed, a delightful, merry laugh that reminded me of the tinkling of a wind chime.

"I am Lilith," she said solemnly, but her eyes were amused.

"Where did you come from?" I managed.

"Does it really matter?" Her hazel eyes told me I should not press for an answer. She had truly beautiful eyes, even larger and more fascinating than Running Deer's. When she looked at me, her eyes were piercing—as if she could see inside me. Absurdly, I found myself feeling that I was the one who was naked.

"What are you doing here . . . like that?" I finally got out.

"You need me," she said simply.

"What?" I fairly exploded. This was getting stranger by the minute. But before I could say anything more, she stepped right up to me and put her hands on my shoulders. Her eyes held me like a bug on a pin. My knees felt wobbly. I noticed her hair was not mixed white and dark like graying hair, but was a uniform, soft gray like some exotic fur. And I smelled her, not perfume but an oddly subtle, attractive fragrance that was powerfully female.

"You do, don't you," she said. It was not a question. "Without me you're stuck right where you are."

Momentarily I was shocked: she seemed to know exactly what I was about. Having become used to such surprises I quickly recovered, only to be caught by the look in her eyes. The love and empathy I saw in them evoked powerful childhood memories. My eyes filled with tears. She reached up and brushed the tears away with her fingers, and her face was soft and concerned.

"I can help you." She began unbuttoning my shirt, but her eyes still looked straight into mine. And without the slightest trace of self-consciousness she said, "Make love to me."

I blushed furiously. Nothing in my experience had prepared me for such an open, direct approach. What do you do with a naked woman who walks up to you in the forest and asks you to make love to her?

There was no way I could have refused her. But in reality, I did not make love to her—she made love to me. Before I knew what had happened I was lying naked on my back in the wet grass and she was all over me. She kissed me ferociously, again and again. I know it's a strange way to put it, but there's no other word to describe it. And when she rubbed against me, her erect nipples left tingling trails across my chest. Then, just about the time I could not stand it any more, she crouched over me and let me slip into her. Lord, what a feeling! It was as though the two of us had become one body, one being. She rode me and I thrust back until I was ready to burst. Then, just as I did, there was a blinding flash and the crackle of a close lightning stroke. Rain began to splash on us, but we were both so hot that several minutes went by before we noticed how cold it was getting. We stroked each other, and she nuzzled her face against my neck, her soft gray hair covering my shoulders and chest.

Finally she got up. "It's cold," she said and without another word led me by the hand over to a spreading spruce tree with a large open space under its lowest branches. She broke off some dead branches from a nearby river willow, her naked body arching beautifully in profile as she stretched on tiptoes to reach the branches she wanted. Using the branches, along with some kind of vine and large leaves from a shrub, she put together a lean-to shelter in a matter of minutes. I marveled at the dexterity and competence she showed in making the thing. All I could do was watch in admiration. When she was finished, she placed the lean-to against the trunk of the spruce tree, and we crawled inside and lay down on the pine needles. They were prickly but dry.

I stroked her back as we lay facing each other. She laughed softly, kissed me—gently this time. I was bursting with questions, but she put her fingers over my lips.

"You know me now. That's enough. When you are ready to know us entirely, you'll have no trouble finding me. Trust me!"

I noticed a secret look of amusement behind her eyes as she said those words. I wanted to ask her what she meant, but the look on her face stopped me. I knew she wouldn't answer any questions. Besides, she had already given me enough. For the first time in my life I knew what union between a man and a woman was really like. Lying there quietly, thinking about how it had been, feeling Lilith caressing my face and body, listening to splattering raindrops and the muttering of the retreating storm, I was soon asleep.

WHEN I AWOKE, perhaps an hour later, it was dark and Lilith was gone. I was disappointed but not surprised. The surprise was finding myself fully dressed and my clothes fairly dry. Lilith must have dressed me, but how could she have done it without waking me? I must have been sleeping like a drunk. All the questions I had thought of earlier ran through my mind. Who was she? Where had she come from? What did she have to do with my grandfather and Running Deer? I stopped short and began thinking about what I did know. I had recently discovered that to be a much more fruitful occupation. For one thing, I knew I had never before seen anyone—male or female—with hair the color of Lilith's. The real question, I decided, was: What was she? In retrospect, the love-making episode and its sequel was beginning to take on the same eerie quality I had come to expect from my previous adventures.

After some consideration I concluded I should stay put for the night and wait for morning to help straighten things out. I nibbled on some beef jerky for a bit, but I wasn't really hungry. Then I just lay there in the lean-to Lilith had built, my mind a maelstrom of seething ideas and memories. I must have lain there thinking for over an hour before drifting off into fitful sleep. I recall waking up several times, but eventually I fell into a deep sleep.

SOMETIME in the middle of the night I suddenly woke up. I found myself sitting bolt upright in the lean-to with beads of sweat all over my face. I felt nervous and my hands were cold and clammy. Through the open front of the shelter I could see stars shining bright and steady. But there was definitely something amiss. My body image felt wrong, almost the way it did the time I woke up in the robot instead of my own body. My senses seemed vaguely dislocated. Then two different perceptions hit me like hammer blows. I realized I was naked again, and at the same time I felt hair on my back. My hair was much too short to reach even my shoulders, let alone my back. For a few seconds my mind reeled under this double onslaught. Then I collected myself, thinking, *So many weird things have already happened to me; surely one more won't make much difference.* Steadying myself, I felt inside my backpack for some matches and lit one. It made an odd, glassy flame that left trails behind as I moved it around. I saw that the hair draped over my shoulders was gray, like Lilith's. Then I got out a small metal mirror from my pack and looked at my face. It was true. There was no longer any doubt about it.

I was in Lilith's body.

My skin crawled, I got goose bumps all over, and waves of nausea ran through me. I felt myself losing control and had to steady myself very deliberately. This was surely the wildest thing that had happened to me yet. What, I thought, could possibly be next? I had not long to wait for an answer.

Abruptly, a gentle calm came over me (if, indeed, I can even refer to myself as *me* under the circumstances). I felt warm and strangely excited. I found I could get into being a woman, even if just for a short time—I felt sure this was merely another weird episode in my pilgrimage. Lying back on the pine needles I luxuriated in my newfound role as a female. I ran my hands all over my body, wondering at the feel of my breasts. I began to feel sensuously alive. Quite to my surprise, I found myself genuinely enjoying this strange new experience.

After what seemed like five or ten minutes of this I noticed a change in the sound of the crickets. Their chirping was getting louder, even strident. The whole chorus began taking on a hollow sound, as though the crickets and I were in a large cave or an amphitheater. The stars were no longer steady but twinkled and shimmered, wavering in their apparent positions as if the sky were threatening to disintegrate.

Then I saw another apparition coming toward me out of the darkness. At first it was just a pale glowing dot in the distance, but it grew slowly and steadily. At length I could make out a human figure, pink and glowing like a phosphorescent sea creature. At first I thought it might be Lilith again. *But how could that be*, I thought, *if I am in her body?* It wasn't Lilith, as it turned out. It was a naked man. I could see him clearly now, and I felt myself strangely excited again. I realized it was a sexual excitement, which seemed odd to me because I have never had any homosexual urges or desires in my life. But I was in a female body now, which was the source of the feelings I was experiencing. As the man drew closer my excitement grew stronger until I found myself writhing with desire. For some reason I found this amusing. When the man got close enough to make out his face, however, I was no longer amused. Not one bit.

The man walking toward me was myself.

My mind reeled again, pushed to the limit by the fantastic situation I was in. I wanted to get up and run away, but my female body wouldn't let me. Instead, I found myself smiling in open sexual invitation—to myself!

What followed is most difficult to relate. How do I describe me making love to myself? I'll have to refer to my male self as he or him for the time being.

Anyway, he came into the lean-to and began stroking my body. To my surprise, this produced waves of pleasure that ran all through me like a slow electric shock. I found myself thinking, So this is what it's like to be the woman! He spoke to me gently, reassuringly, and with a shock I recognized the voice as Lilith's. His stroking drove me wild. I began writhing in his arms. I felt my taut nipples rubbing against him and wondered if he was feeling the same sensations that I had just the afternoon before when Lilith made love to me.

The strangest part of all began when he entered me. It was like in the afternoon only much stronger. This time we became one in consciousness as well as body. He was part of me. I was part of him. We were in a universe all our own, seemingly weightless. I found I could experience myself as either the man making love to the woman, or the woman making love to the man. This gradually became fused into one, until I was both male and female at the same time. And I believe this consciousness was shared with Lilith. We were somehow merged in a wonderful cosmic rhapsody.

THE END seemed slow in coming. It began as a gentle vibration like the stroking of a taut violin string. Somewhere in the depths of me—of us—this feeling grew and grew until it dominated everything. Suspended as it were in a nameless void, I got the image of a giant cosmic whirlpool: millions of stars whirling ever faster and faster into a tighter and tighter vortex. Soon the shrieking of our bodies increased to an unbearable pitch. Something snapped under the strain and a silent explosion went off in the depths of our being. In that instant I became like a rocket bursting in multi-colored splendor across the sky, and then abruptly, with a tremendous feeling of relief, falling in ashes to the ground. For a brief moment the lines of an almost-forgotten poem ran through my mind:

> *Softly I fall, divided like snowflakes,*
> *Reborn in the silvery shards*
> *Of ten thousand shattered stars,*
> *Silently reclaiming the forgotten void.*

Then a sweet, relaxing warmth spread swiftly throughout my body, followed by a wave of darkness that brought release from everything. My last thought was, *If dying is like this it won't be hard to take.*

Our spiritual friend does not wear any armor at all;
  he is a naked person.
Compared with his nakedness, we are wearing cement.

—Chogyam Trungpa,
Cutting Through Spiritual Materialism

7

The Guru

A wakening early the next morning, I found brilliant sunshine flooding in on me through the open face of the lean-to. Once again I was fully clothed and in my own body. The relief I felt was oddly mixed with an echo of disappointment that seemed to come from the depths of my being. I shook my head and stretched, trying to clear the cobwebs from my mind. Birds were singing and the sky was a brilliant azure blue, making everything look like an overly sharp Kodachrome. In the brightness of the morning the events of the previous afternoon and night seemed unreal in retrospect. But they were all too real.

While I was thinking about this I became aware of a faint sizzle, soon followed by the smell of bacon cooking. Thinking *Now what?* I crawled out of the lean-to. I found Lilith, cooking bacon over a small campfire. She was dressed in cut-off shorts and a blouse of some soft, pale yellow material, open down the middle and tied together in a knot just above her navel. I thought she was the most beautiful thing I had ever seen.

"Hello," she said softly. I noted a look of respect in her eyes, a look that had not been there yesterday. I wondered why.

"Hello," I answered back. "I'm glad you're here."

She looked me straight in the eye and spoke with conviction.

"I'll always be here for you. You'll always be here for me. That's the way it is."

Somewhat to my surprise I found myself silently assenting to this. Bold and confident, I took her in my arms, kissed her gently on the lips. Quick and warm, she responded as though our bond of love had the strength of many moons.

"Who are you, Lilith? Who are you, really?" I asked, holding her in my arms, reluctant to let go.

"I am your complement and your alter ego," she replied. "I am your guru."

"But have you no identity of your own?" I countered.

She laughed her merry wind-chime laugh.

"Of course, you silly man! We complete each other. You are my alter ego, my guru. I found you last night, just as you found me last night. We found each other and we found ourselves. Now we are both completed. We are a perfect pair because we perfect each other."

"Together we make God as we make love," I murmured, recalling the line from *The Purloined God*. "But how can I be your guru? I don't know enough to be a guru."

"You know me," she replied, laughing again. "Don't sell yourself short. You know a great deal more than you realize. You are the perfect guru for me, as I am for you."

"Okay," I responded, deciding to put her to the test, "then what about last night? In the middle of the night I woke up in your body, you came to me in my body, and we made love together—mad, passionate love, as they say. Was that real?"

She smiled and pressed up against me until her face was just inches from mine.

"Didn't it feel like it was real?"

I had to admit that it did. The memory caused me to shiver from recalled ecstasy.

"But did it actually happen?" I pressed.

She looked at me thoughtfully, as if calculating whether I was ready to hear what she had to say next.

"That depends," she replied. "If you mean, did it happen as a physically observable event that could have been seen by someone else, the answer is no. But if you mean, was the experience real, then the answer is yes—absolutely. It did happen to you, and it did happen to me. It happened to us and only to us."

"Wow!" I exclaimed, enthralled. "I see what you mean. Our experience came from shared consciousness, not from any physical exchange. So it was real only for us. Anyone else would have seen only a man and a woman making love."

She laughed softly and hugged me.

"And you say you don't know enough to be my guru!"

What could I say? I saw immediately what she meant. Yet I had no idea how such a thing could happen, and I said so.

"Neither have I," she admitted. "But I know one thing for sure: I'm glad it happened. I found I needed it just as badly as you did. I was stuck, too, and I didn't even know it. Besides, we were terrific together—both times."

I blushed, not being used to such directness. Then by unspoken agreement we sat down to eat the breakfast Lilith had prepared. It was good.

"Black Buffalo!" Lilith said so abruptly I almost dropped the bacon I was eating. "Your name is Black Buffalo."

"But I told you, my name is . . ." I started, but she cut me short.

"I know. That's your ordinary name. I'm talking about your Indian name. It tells who you are and where you came from. The Buffalo is from the north, the place of wisdom or knowledge. The blackness tells that you have gone west, which is the looks-within place: introspection. Don't you see now?—that's why we comple-ment each other so beautifully. My Indian name is Yellow Mouse. The mouse comes from the south, the place of innocence. The yel-low tells that I have gone to the east—the sees-far place, or the place of illumination. You see now? We each have just what the other one needs for completion."

I nodded my head tentatively, for this was all new to me. Yet I saw what she had said made sense even though it was a strange new way for me.

"Together we make a medicine wheel, a completed shield," she added. "I think you and I will know each other for a long time."

I smiled broadly. "I certainly hope we will. You are the most fascinating woman I've ever met."

"And you are the man," she said cryptically, smiling again like the rising sun.

It was quickly settled: from that day forward we would seek our destiny together. I felt buoyantly joyful. For the first time since I had left my grandfather's house I believed I knew both where I was going and how I was getting there. What a glorious day that was for us! Together we had broken through the cracks of our own private worlds into a much grander universe that lay beyond. Nei-ther of us could restrain the joy that filled our hours as we began our journey together, walking hand in hand.

I can't overstate the strength of the bond between Lilith and me. There was never any talk of marriage. We knew we had been mar-ried by God, or by the universe, that night in Beaver Valley. It was irrevocable and we both knew it.

As we went on our way together we compared notes. It soon became obvious that until yesterday our paths had been very dif-ferent. Mine had consisted of tremendous shocks to the integrity of my world of knowledge, which at length resulted in my looking inward, just as Lilith had diagnosed. Her path had comprised equally jarring shocks to her world of innocence, which led her to begin looking at things in a new way—the 'sees-far' place, as she put it. We had come together—obviously not by accident—at the precise moment when our formerly divergent paths crossed. Joined now, we aimed toward a new dawn, a new awakening.

It would not be long in coming.

WE HAD BEEN WALKING together for some time in silence. I was thinking about the events of the past couple of days when Lilith interrupted my thoughts.

"What's so amusing?"

"I was just thinking how judgmental I was last week when I realized Vadid and Running Deer were making love. Now I'm in the same situation."

"Does that bother you?" she asked.

"I guess it does a bit," I admitted.

"Why?" Lilith pressed. "Are you hung up on the old Biblical 'Thou shalt not commit adultery' bit?"

"I'm not really sure. I guess it's because society judges adultery as bad. But I'm sure it stems from the Bible in the beginning."

"The Bible," she announced as if changing the subject, "is a really heavy book, and there's lots of truth in what it says. But you've got to remember it was written by men, men who were not beyond adding things on their own, things their God would never have told them. And believe it or not the adultery thing is one of them. Actually, all of the repressive things the Bible says about sex are a bunch of malarkey."

"Go on," I prompted her, "this is interesting. Do you know the true story?"

"Well, I know part of it," she began. "But in order for you to understand what I mean, I'll have to back up some and start at the beginning—in Genesis, actually."

"Shoot!"

"Genesis," she continued, "says man was created in the image of God. Do you believe that?"

"Not if it means God looks like a human being, I don't."

"Good!" she said, smiling. "You're absolutely right. That's not what it means at all. The image is conceptual, not concrete. It's allegorical. I took a long course in the Bible once. We were taught never to take the Bible out of its historical context, and that's what the context was—allegory. The whole Bible is like that, especially the Old Testament. For example, where it says God forms man out of the dust and breathes the breath of life into him, it means just that—but not in the ordinary way of thinking about it. I mean, you don't see God come along, make a mud pie, and then breathe life into it. That's not what it means."

"What does it mean, then?" I asked, curious.

"Well, just think about it. When you were formed inside your mother's womb, where do you suppose the substance for your body came from?"

"My mother's body," I replied.

"Okay, but where did she get it from?"

"From food, of course."

"Aha! And where did the food come from?"

"Animals and plants?"

"Of course," she replied. "But from what source did they get their substance?"

"Well, animals get theirs ultimately from plants. And plants get their substance from . . . from the ground!"

"Exactly!" she exclaimed, triumphantly. "See? You did come from the dust, just as the Bible says. And where did your first breath come from? Why did you take it?"

"Instinct. You take your first breath instinctively."

"Yes," she agreed, "exactly! And if you're willing to grant that God created all of this, you must agree it was He who put that instinct in you in the first place. So wasn't it God who breathed the breath of life into you?"

"I guess so," I replied, laughing. "I'm beginning to see what you mean. The Bible really does have to be read more carefully than I used to believe."

"Great! Now we're really getting somewhere. Okay—let's go back to the image of God. Let's see . . . you told me a while back you recently discovered that the world you experience is one you yourself create out of nerve impulses, and as far as you know there is no way you can experience the world directly. Right?"

"Right," I agreed.

"Okay—then we're at the first point of similarity: God creates the universe and each human being creates a replica of that universe for his or her own experiencing. That's an image of God: you create your world in an image of the way God does it."

"Yes!" I exclaimed. "I came to the same conclusion myself because of some experiences I've had on my pilgrimage. I create my own world just as God creates the universe."

"Good," she answered, "then you're ready for the next step—the unity of God. All the great religions teach that God is one; there is no duality in God. On a human level this principle is imaged in sexual intercourse. Intercourse is the joining of opposites. In sexual union the yin and yang of the universe are merged. Remember what you said earlier today? 'Together we make God as we make love'? It means that in sexual union we form an image of God as completed yin and yang."

"Of course!" I answered in rising excitement. "That's why we were able to exchange consciousness and experience each other's bodies last night."

"Yes, something like that."

"And there's more?"

"Yes. Lots more. I'm not sure you're ready for some of it, and there's even more I don't understand yet."

"Try me," I said, hoping she would tell me more.

"Okay, we just covered the second point of similarity. The third point is more subtle, or at least harder to understand. It has to do with dreaming."

"Dreaming?" I asked incredulously. "What could dreaming have to do with it?"

"Plenty!" she smiled as she spoke. "Let me start with a question. How good are you at imitating other people?"

"Lousy," I replied with a broad grin. "I couldn't fool anyone."

"Suppose I said you can and do imitate others perfectly, so well that you can fool even yourself."

"I'd begin to wonder about your sanity," I replied with a friendly smile, unwilling to risk any discord.

"That's what most people say," she replied. "Tell me something else, then: Have you ever dreamed about your mother or father?"

"Of course I have. Hasn't everyone?"

"I suppose so," Lilith agreed. "But tell me: When you dream about your parents, or a brother or sister, or a close friend, are they perfectly recognizable?"

"Yes, of course they . . . " I broke off, a feeling of consternation overtaking me.

"Aha!" she said. "I see by the look on your face that you're catching on. Of course—where did you think those other people in your dreams came from? You made them all—each and every one of them. You imitated them perfectly because you were the one who made them up in the first place, right? You're the one who creates your world, the world that you experience."

"Of course! Why didn't I realize that before?"

"Probably because you never thought about it."

"Okay—but what does this have to do with God?"

"A fair question," she acknowledged, laughing her merry wind-chime laugh I so enjoyed. "To see the answer, we need to look at the way the world's great religions portray God and the universe. Basically, they say that God, having created the universe, has fallen asleep and is dreaming He is seven billion different people. Folks hear this and ask, *But how can we all be the same person and not know it?* The answer to that is locked in our dream worlds. We might just as well ask, How can we dream we are all these different people and not know it? We may not know the answer to the question, but we know it happens, because it happens to us all."

"Yes, I see that," I agreed. "But how . . . ?"

"I'm getting to that," she broke in. "But first we have to look at the way we dream. First, there's the dreamer—that's us, in a form of simple consciousness. We're not self conscious in dreams, because if we were we would know we were dreaming, and that seldom happens. Next, there's the part of us that does the dreaming, that orchestrates the dream, so to speak. This is obviously a higher level within us, because it is above the level of the dreamer. Let's call this part the 'dream agent' for lack of a better term. Finally, we have the whole human being, which contains both the dreamer and the dream agent, as well as the dream itself and the rest of the dream characters. You with me so far?"

I nodded, transfixed by the picture she was drawing for me.

"Okay," she continued, "see what that means: The dreamer—the dreaming person—is made in the image of God because he or she images the way the universe works. Remember, the Bible says that through Christ all things are created. Okay, so Christ is the dream agent of the universe. He dreams the dream and plays all the parts. But like the dreamer, each of us is unaware of this and thinks he or she is a separate entity, like the characters in our own dreams, which we perceive as others although we play each and every one of them ourselves. The people in this universe are the dreamers, the characters in the dream. And the whole thing—the dreaming person—is God. That's the third point of similarity. In our dreams we image the workings of the universe, which is God. We're made in the image of God."

"Wow!" I exclaimed, stunned. Then I thought of a disparity.

"But in our dreams the dreamer is unique, more real than the dream characters."

"Yes," she agreed, "that is one point of departure. We can only be ourselves one at a time; God can be all of us at once—because He is God. But that doesn't really change anything; the dreamer can be thought of as each of us taken one at a time. If I am the subject, then I am the dreamer. If you're the subject, then you are the dreamer. And so forth. In each of these separate dreams, the subject is the dreamer and the rest of us are dream characters; but each of us—including the dreamer—is played by Christ, or Cosmic Consciousness, if you prefer."

"Oh, then this isn't just a Christian interpretation?"

"No, of course not. It's universal. Each religion has some form of this embedded in its mythology."

"And this Cosmic Consciousness you speak of, is it the same thing Bucke wrote about in his book *Cosmic Consciousness*?"

"Precisely. You've read it?"

I nodded assent.

"Then you're several steps ahead of most people at this stage. I'm sure you noticed that Bucke believed self consciousness is never attained in the dream state."

"Yes, and I disagree, because I have experienced self consciousness in dreams. Once, a long time ago, I dreamt of a sea serpent swimming in a large lake, something like the Loch Ness monster. It frightened me until I realized, *This is my dream. I can make it go away if I want to.* So I stared at it until—Poof!—it disappeared. I relaxed, and—Pop!—there it was again. I made it disappear a few more times after that, and then my dream agent changed the scene on me and I never saw it again.

"More recently, I dreamt of a pretty young woman I was walking down a street with. Suddenly I realized I was dreaming, so I reached out and touched her on the shoulder and said, 'I know I'm dreaming.' Instantly her face changed, turning rapidly into that of a rather plain, middle-aged woman. Then she faded away completely and I woke up."

"My, you have interesting dreams!" Lilith exclaimed. "I see you also made the connection that knowing you are dreaming implies a self-conscious state. That helps a lot with what I want to say next. You see, the coming of self consciousness in a dream is the image of the coming of Cosmic Consciousness in the waking state. With self consciousness, the dreamer knows he is dreaming; that is, he sees the true nature of the reality of his dream world. With the coming of Cosmic Consciousness a person sees the true nature of reality. Such a person becomes Christ Conscious. It's the only way we can experience the outside world directly, without the intervention of our own self-created world, which is such a necessary part of ordinary perception."

"Has that ever happened to you?" I asked, intensely interested in this new direction of our conversation.

"No," she admitted. "But I certainly hope it does some day."

"Me, too," I agreed. "Ever since I read Bucke I've hoped something like that might happen to me. I've always wondered what it would be like."

"Just another thing we have in common," she replied, laughing gently. "By the way, do you know why Adam and Eve got thrown out of the garden of Eden, and where the garden is?"

"They got thrown out for eating some kind of fruit God had told them not to eat, but I have no idea where the Garden of Eden is."

"Actually," Lilith explained, "they got tossed out for becoming self conscious. Look at what Genesis says: The fruit they ate was from the Tree of the Knowledge of Good and Evil. Only self conscious beings like us have a sense of good and evil. Animals, which are in a state of simple consciousness, have no such sense. And look what happened after Adam and Eve ate that fruit: they became aware of their nakedness and covered up. When God came back, He asked them 'Who told you that you were naked?'

He knew they must have eaten the forbidden fruit because they had become ashamed of their nakedness. A simple-conscious being would not be ashamed of its nakedness, or even be aware of it. Animals aren't aware that they are naked."

"True," I agreed. "So where is the Garden of Eden?"

"Well," she continued, "the Garden of Eden is just an allegory for the state of innocence that is experienced by simple-conscious beings. Animals still live in the Garden of Eden. So where is it? Look around you—it's everywhere."

"I see! It's not a place, it's a state of consciousness."

"Right you are. And once you become self conscious you can never return to your former state of innocence. So, you are, in effect, locked out of the garden.

"Also, this answers the question: 'Where did the wives of Abel and Cain come from?' Adam and Eve were not the only two human beings in the world. They were the first two *self conscious* humans. The wives of Abel and Cain would have come from those women who were still in a simple-conscious state."

"Yes, that makes sense," I said, beginning to see how all the crazy things I had experienced since I had left my grandfather's house were beginning to fit together. "Lilith, you're a really heavy person, you know?"

She laughed, and this time she sounded like a wind chime in a storm. Then she fell abruptly serious.

"You bring out the best in me, you really do," she said, adding, "In every way."

I blushed again, and we walked on in silence.

Swiftly arose and spread around me the peace and joy and
knowledge that pass all the art and argument of the earth;
And I know that the hand of God is the elderhand of my own,
And I know that the spirit of God is the eldest brother
of my own.

—Walt Whitman, "Song of Myself"
from *Leaves of Grass*, 1855 edition

8
The Son Also Rises

s LILITH AND I continued our journey to nowhere in particular I gradually realized just how much I had learned in the few short weeks since leaving my grandfather's house. By now I knew that the world is largely an illusion and what we call matter does not really exist—it is just energy confined to form. I also had discovered that our very existence is largely an illusion. We are not what we think we are. I had come to see time itself as just another of these illusions with no independent existence of its own. In reality it is only another physical dimension. Yet these were mere matters of knowledge, important only to my own progress. The really significant things I had learned were about myself, and about all of us. The victories over others I had celebrated during my life, all the petty little advantages and examples of one-upmanship, I now recognized as my worst defeats, and I saw that the setbacks I had suffered at the hands of an unthinking, unfeeling world and had overcome and learned from were actually my greatest victories.

What a topsy-turvy world this has become, I mused as I contemplated these things. I have come to realize that I cannot hurt
others by my actions; I can injure only myself. I have discovered I
can accomplish nothing in this world by acting on external
objects, yet do everything by working on myself. I can only love
myself through the love I have for others, and the only way I can
love others is by allowing them to love me.

Then one day I realized I had lost my sense of sin. After all, the
things I had done to hurt others really hurt only me; my sins were
against myself and were already charged to my own account. I had
already borrowed the price of their redemption in karma. The
wrongs I could remember having committed were like ghosts now,
pale images without substance. I was free now, really free.

But when I contemplated my newfound freedom, I found there
was nothing to do with it. I no longer had any desire for material
possessions, which had never held a strong attraction for me anyway. As for power, the ambition to control others or be admired by
them, I never had wanted it and the idea was now totally repug-
nant. My only wish now was that in some way I could communicate
to others my exceedingly great fortune so they, too, might become
free as I was, no longer bound to the wheel of karma and death.
But I knew this desire was also illusory; there was no way I could
effect the salvation of those around me.

STILL LATER I BECAME AWARE THAT I had not yet accomplished
everything I might. Even though I knew these things and had
experienced most of them firsthand, my knowledge was intellectual.
I had not realized these things in my own being. The final step on
the path I had taken still eluded my grasp. And I knew why: unlike
knowledge this self-realization cannot be acquired, it is not a thing
to be grasped. I knew I must wait for it to happen if it were to happen at all. I resolved to be patient and put out of my mind this
change I craved, so I might be receptive to it rather than be so bent

on desiring it that I would end up blocking the very thing that I wanted so badly.

You might think by then I should have known I would not have long to wait.

A FEW DAYS LATER Lilith and I came to a quiet little village in a green valley. The place looked peaceful and serene, and yet I could not shake a feeling of foreboding that had come over me from almost the instant I had first caught sight of it. I had no wish to create bad karma where perhaps there was none and kept my tongue. But eventually I confided my feelings to Lilith.

"Brrr!" I shivered involuntarily. "Why do I feel as if something awful is about to happen here?"

"You too?" she replied. "I thought there was something wrong with me."

"If there is, then it's a *folie à deux*." She cast a sharp glance at me when I said this, but made no reply.

As we entered the village in silence, each of us wondered whether something evil were really going to happen and, if so, how bad it was going to be. I suppose we should have had more faith in our own psychic abilities at that point. In any event, we pressed on into the center of the place, watchful and alert. Before long one of the townspeople spied us coming, took an instant liking to us, and insisted we have lunch with him in his outdoor cafe. This man, a jolly round fellow who reminded me of Charles Laughton, no sooner had served the meal than he began to regale us with stories about some of the local characters. He quickly had us both laughing so hard we had trouble eating the delicious food he had put on our plates. Before long we had entirely forgotten about our earlier premonitions of trouble.

The ruckus that suddenly exploded out of a nearby side street therefore caught us off guard. A rag-tag boy perhaps fifteen years old came running across the street heading, apparently, for an alley next to the cafe where we were eating. He was pursued by a crowd of angry people, mostly adults and all yelling like banshees. The unfortunate youngster tripped on the lip of the driveway leading into the alley and went sprawling on the sidewalk about twenty feet from where we sat. Before he could get up the mob was upon him. Some of them held his hands and feet while others beat on his face and chest and a few seemed to be trying to rip the clothes off him. Lilith and I were horrified. We looked at each other, nodded mutual assent, and quickly walked over to the edge of the crowd.

"What has this boy done for you to treat him so?" I thundered in what I hoped was my most authoritative tone of voice. Quite to my surprise, they immediately stopped attacking the poor boy and looked at me as though I were a policeman or some other authority. I knew I would have to act quickly before the effect wore off, lest they should turn their anger on me.

"He's a no-good, that's what he is," replied the one who had been beating the boy the most enthusiastically. "He's never done nothin' good in his whole life. And you know what he's done now? He stole the widow Clifford's purse, that's what he done. Pushed her over in her wheelchair, he did. Knocked her clean out. Mebbe she's dead, for all we know." The others chimed in their assent to these statements. One middle-aged woman held out a small brown leather purse toward me.

"See for yourself, stranger. This here's the widow's purse. We caught him with it in his hand. Walkin' right down the street with it, he was. He didn't even try to hide it, neither."

I looked at the boy's face and read terror but no guilt. I looked over to Lilith for confirmation, but she was looking across the street at a large, husky girl wearing an oddly feminine peasant dress. I saw what had caught Lilith's eye: the girl was obviously very interested in what was happening but did not want to get too close. There was pain in the girl's eyes, a message we both read easily. But it was Lilith who moved first, striding across the street and looking right into the girl's eyes. She said nothing, but continuing to look at the girl she reached out slowly and took her by the hand. Without a word, but with a look of some relief, the girl followed Lilith's lead across the street to where the rest of us were standing.

"This young lady has something to tell you," she announced to the crowd; then turning to the girl she said, "Go ahead. I promise, no one will hurt you."

"He didn't do it," she said dully, looking on the verge of tears. "I did it. I didn't mean no harm. I needed the money for a ticket to the dance. Nobody asked me. I was just gonna grab the purse and run, but when I grabbed it, she held on and tried to pull it out of my hands, and I fell and knocked the wheelchair over. I didn't mean to hurt her, honest. But Tommy—he saw what I did and chased me. He caught me, too, and took the purse away from me. He said he was gonna give it back to the widow and I didn't have any right to it. He said it was wrong to take things that belong to other people. You all say he never does nothin' good, but he was the one who was right. He tried to do something good, not me. If you're gonna beat on somebody, you should be beatin' on me, not him."

She turned and clung to Lilith, crying quietly, thoroughly ashamed of herself. The others evidently felt the same way because they silently began to disperse. One of the men pulled the boy to his feet, brushed the dust from his clothes, and said "Sorry" in a gruff but kindly tone of voice. The boy said nothing; he only looked relieved at escaping without any real harm. He looked up at the two of us.

"Thanks. I don't know what to say. You guys saved my ass ... er, my life, I mean."

"It was nothing," I said, and meant it. But on reflection I guess I'd have to say it was more than that. The boy could have been badly hurt—for no reason, as it turned out—had it not been for the ability both Lilith and I now possessed to read the faces of others quickly and accurately. Not everyone has that faculty, not by a long shot. Had Lilith and I not happened by when we did, who knows what terrible tragedy might have ensued?

Then, just about the time we turned to resume our interrupted meal, I noticed Lilith's face. It was radiant. She seemed to glow with an inner light brighter than the noonday sun. I mentioned it, but she only blushed slightly and said something about finishing our lunch.

I couldn't get it out of my mind though. All afternoon as we walked I kept stealing secret glances at her face. That strange, subtle glow was always there. I began to get the same feeling I had gotten so many times before as a precursor to one of my mind-blowing experiences. I tried to shake it but I couldn't.

THAT EVENING we made camp in a meadow of lush, deep grass nestled among rolling hills. As the sun sank and shadows began to creep across the land I noticed Lilith's glow did not diminish as I had half expected it would but instead seemed to increase, growing stronger as the daylight grew weaker.

"That moon glow from you is getting brighter by the minute," I remarked playfully.

"Maybe I'm just reflecting some of the light you're giving off."

"Me? What are you talking about?"

"Go look in a mirror if you don't believe me." She laughed her merry wind-chime laugh at my sudden consternation.

Somewhat nervously I poked around in my knapsack until I found the small hand mirror. I held it up in front of my face and with a shock I saw she was right. My face was glowing too. It was nothing pronounced, just that my face was brighter than anything else in the mirror. I felt the hairs rising on the back of my neck. I thought, *Oh, no! Here we go again!*

Lilith's voice interrupted my thoughts.

"Come, my beloved," she called softly.

I turned around and saw her standing there in the gathering dusk, naked. Her whole body glowed, her limbs only faintly, her trunk, neck, and head, more brightly. The brightest glow ran in a crescendo from her navel to her head, and her face was almost too bright to look at. Her hair, normally a pale, uniform gray, looked dark and mysterious against her glowing, translucent skin. What a vision of loveliness!

"Come!" she repeated, holding her hands out palms upward as if in supplication.

I shivered a bit because of what was happening to us, but as usual I was so drawn to her it did not matter. I held her in my arms and kissed her. When I opened my eyes, I was surprised to see her glowing had increased perceptibly during our kiss. But she spoke first.

"My god!" she whispered. "You look like a comet."

I looked at my arms. They were glowing noticeably now. I undressed, and as I did so I found my whole body was glowing just as hers was.

"What's happening to us?" I asked, somewhat lamely.

"I don't know, but whatever it is I want to enjoy it. You ask too many questions."

"I know," I admitted. It was true. I was always the one to ask questions, always the one to want to know the whys and where-fores. I quickly resolved to stop asking questions and just enjoy the experience we were having for what it was.

We began to make love together, softly, gently, more slowly and deliberately than we ever had before. As we did it was as if God were there watching our every move. (And friend, if you don't think that's a turn-on, then you have much to learn about that subject.) Every time we touched each other our bodies would glow more brightly at the point of contact. As we became more passion-ate our bodies began to throb and pulsate with light and energy. Waves of warmth came from deep within us and rushed to our skin, dissipating there in pulses of light that lit up the meadow grass around us.

When I entered her (or did she enter me?) the real magic began. I saw her skin become transparent and inside, under her skin, I began to see a being of light that only with great difficulty I recognized as an image of myself. Lilith was having the same experience. You may well wonder how I knew this at the time. You see, we each became the other, just as we had several times before. But this time was different—more real, more definite. It wasn't that I just experienced being her, or did so to the exclusion of being myself as I had once before in Beaver Valley. No, I became her and me at the same time, and she likewise. We became each other.

Instead of the two becoming one, the one became two.

I was the eternal female, opening myself to my lover, urging him into me. At the same time I was the eternal male, holding my lover against me, thrusting myself into her, possessing her and myself at one and the same time. We spoke not a word, for no words were necessary; we thought in unison, and our thoughts became us.

As our passion built toward its God-given climax, we became aware we were dreaming. Not that we actually were dreaming, but the sensation was akin to becoming self conscious while dreaming. We were becoming aware in some indefinable yet undeniable way that we were not really awake. As this happened we found we were also becoming conscious of the psyches of others, many others. First it was those we knew, then those we knew of, and finally it was a great crowd, a veritable babbling mass of humanity. We experienced the minds of everyone at once. And not just *experienced*—we were them, we became them. We were ourselves and them at the same time.

And then we began to awaken. As our greatly-expanded consciousness seemed to grow without limit, we soon became aware of a vast over-psyche, a mind of minds, if you will, that was also us. Again, it was as if we had been dreaming and, beginning to awaken, were becoming aware of ourselves as the dream agent rather than just the dreamers. We enjoyed a strange sense of dual identity where at first the mind of minds was our alter ego, then increasingly we became the mind of minds, the dream agent, and our alter ego became our ordinary self. We became aware that a part of us was dreaming me and another part was dreaming Lilith, but we were no longer directly connected to these dreams. The higher we got, the stronger the sense of being this mind of minds was, and the weaker and less important became the minds of others, even of we ourself (for we were no longer separate selves).

The final moment of climax was an unbearable, wrenching explosion that at last propelled us into the state for which we both had been waiting so long. The final bond had been broken, and we now merged with the mind of minds, all connection to our body (or bodies) and our earthly existence severed. All that we had formerly only known we now saw and felt and savored. There was no environment in which we then existed; we were the universe and the universe was us. We became pure joy. I know that's not much of a description, but it's the only one I can come up with. Where we were, what we were, was beyond words. Using language to express this would be like trying to describe rainbows to the blind. But one thing I do know: in those brief minutes (or was it hours?) we learned more than either of us had in all the years we had lived on this puny earth. The universe was within us, and the earth was to us an insignificant atom, like a mote in God's eye.

We had become the Son of God, and through us was everything made that has being. We were making everything new, and everything *is* new. Since then we both can say, "Before Abraham was, I am," and mean it. It's true, you know. I—we—you—have always been and always shall be. Time is not real. Only our being—the Son of God with amnesia, if you will—only that being, our being, His being, is real. All else is illusion. And all the kings and queens of earth are like children making sand castles on the beach and then arguing and fighting over which castle belongs to whom while the tide rushes in. Truly, truly, could the Son of man say,

"You are like children playing in the market place, saying, 'We piped and you did not dance; we wept and you did not mourn.'"

Men are like caterpillars arguing over their own greatness when it is really the butterfly that is important, not the caterpillar. The sons and daughters of man must die before they can live. They must die to their false selves before they can be born as their real Self, just as the caterpillar must 'die' and become that living sarcophagus we call a chrysalis, from which a butterfly will eventually emerge in all its glory.

I am at peace now; Lilith and I are at peace now. We are both as you see me today. We no longer try to do anything. We take things as they come, letting today's trouble be sufficient for today. We do not try to save anyone, for no one wants to be saved and it is impossible to save anyone even if we should wish to do so. We turn no one away who wants to learn, for that is why we are here—all of us. But to those who ask we teach that one learns only from his own experience, not from the teachings of others. Another may lead you to the still waters, but you must drink of them for yourself.

And so it was that Lilith and I returned together to my grandfather's house, and I told him all that had happened to me, and to us. And just as I told you in the beginning, he said I was mad. What he actually said was, "Thank God, you have finally become a madman!" When I asked him what he meant by that, he said it came from the writings of Herman Hesse. He told me I had experienced what Hesse called "The Magic Theatre." Hesse, he said, wrote that it was for madmen only.

Perhaps it is. And then again, perhaps it is not....

And this is our life, exempt from public haunt,
Finds tongues in trees, books in the running brooks,
Sermons in stones, and good in everything.

—William Shakespeare,
As You Like It, Act 2, Scene 1

Epilogue

The last time I saw Beelzebub's grandson Lilith was with him. We met by chance (??) at *La Cueva* one summer's eve when the soft shroud of dusk had already descended upon the land. Even so, I saw them both plainly. Lilith was every bit as striking as the description I have recorded on these pages, and then some. True, I have seen women whose facial features are more perfectly arranged than hers. But never have I met a woman who made a deeper impression on me. She is statuesque, standing almost my height without heels. Her soft gray hair is truly exotic. I have seen nothing like it in all my experience in this life. The inner beauty and sheer force of her personality overwhelm mere physical reality and make her appear more beautiful than she is objectively. When she took my hand in greeting, I got the impression that energy flowed from her touch into my body. And those eyes! I thought Beelzebub's grandson had incredible eyes until I met Lilith. There is no way I could adequately describe them, and I shall make no attempt to do so. Suffice it to say that looking into her eyes is even more of a trip than looking into his. Lilith and he are, indeed, a most perfectly matched couple.

We passed a few minutes discussing things of common interest. When Lilith suddenly laughed at one of my remarks, her laughter reminded me, too, of the tinkling of a wind chime. I am certain she would be very easy to love.

Beelzebub's grandson told me he had felt the need to see me again so he could give me something. He handed me the dog-eared copy of *The Purloined God* that Vadid had given him. I felt deeply honored by this gift.

OUR CONVERSATION that evening was of no consequence so far as this little book is concerned, and therefore not important to you, the reader. But I do want to tell you about the appearance of this strange couple. As it grew ever darker their faces did not dim proportionally. I shivered when I realized I was seeing a minor display of the kind of inner light that Beelzebub's grandson had described to me. By the time we parted company their faces were clearly glowing in the dark, looking for all the world as though they had been coated with luminescent paint. Reluctantly, I turned and walked away. The gathering darkness forced me to use a flashlight to see my way. Yet when I turned to take a final look at Lilith and her friend, I saw them making their way confidently without any artificial lighting. Even at some distance I could see a distinct glow emanating from their heads.

I was impressed.

∼ ✿ ∼

So, where do we stand now? That depends on you. You have read the book (unless you're like me and skip around a lot, in which case desist—none of this will make any sense to you yet). Possibly you are one of those who will have been offended by the implication that the use of psychedelic 'drugs' can advance one spiritually. Let's face it, government mishandling of the drug problem and media scare tactics have turned drugs into the witch hunt of the late twentieth century. Not all of this hysteria is unwarranted. Many drugs are dangerous and should be kept out of the hands of the general public. But not at the expense of making the victim a criminal. And that is precisely what the present anti-drug laws are doing. Drugs are bad because they ruin peoples lives (so goes the party line) therefore we outlaw them. And because they are outlawed, anyone who possesses them becomes a criminal. But this includes the very ones the law was intended to protect. So the anti-drug laws join the laws against suicide among those absurd statutes that result in the persecution of those they were intended to protect. Seems like Alice in Wonderland logic, doesn't it?

Not only that, but consider the above premise: Drugs ruin people's lives. Is it true? No, of course not. But we human beings always want something external to blame our troubles on. "My child isn't bad. It was those evil drugs that led him astray." It could not possibly be the child's fault, could it? You hear it said that cocaine killed Len Bias. Nonsense! Len Bias killed Len Bias— unless you are prepared to believe that the cocaine leapt out of its container and forced its way into his body. To paraphrase the notorious National Rifle Association: Drugs don't kill people, people kill people. Whatever became of sin?

On television we saw a stern-faced Peter Jennings solemnly asking us, "Would you want your surgeon operating on you when he was high?" I don't know. Would I? Not if he was high on alcohol. No way! But other drugs? It would depend on the circumstances. In any event, many people have been operated on by a surgeon who was high whether they wanted it or not. Dr. William Stewart Halsted, one of the founding surgeons of Johns Hopkins Hospital and widely known as the father of modern surgery, was a morphine addict from the age of thirty-four to the day of his death. He operated upon hundreds of patients and gained world renown for his skill. Only a select few were privy to the facts of his addiction until several years after his death. There have been other such examples, but his is the best known. So what is the answer to Peter's question? You tell me.

In any event, I wish to make it plain that the references to the use of such substances in this book are to the aptly-named psyche-delic (mind-manifesting) drugs only. John Lennon once remarked that he never would have found God had it not been for pot (cannabis). Upon hearing of his remark, Queen Elizabeth is said to have commented that it was an awful thing for Mr. Lennon to say. When asked by a reporter about her remark, Lennon retorted that he had his act together, let the queen get hers together. I agree with John Lennon. People should refrain from making comments on subjects they know nothing about. And believe me, those who have never experienced psychedelics know nothing about them. *Nothing at all.*

Make no mistake, however: You will get nowhere abusing any substance, and many will get you nowhere even if you don't abuse them. This applies especially to the legal drugs (caffeine, tobacco, alcohol) and the narcotics (codeine, morphine, heroin) which are entirely useless in this respect. Stimulants are virtually useless. On-ly the psychedelics—cannabis, peyote (mescaline), psilocybin (from sacred mushrooms), and LSD—are of any use, and these only if used in a spiritual way.

I can't recommend this for anyone.

Oh, and by the way—don't ever drink battery acid. And never light a match to see if there is any fuel in your gas tank.

~ ❁ ~

Now that you have read this book, did you understand it? Unless you are incredibly lucky, or were in the 'right place' already, the answer is: probably not.

So what are you to make of this book? That, too, is entirely up to you.

Richard Bach, the author of *Jonathan Livingston Seagull*, once wrote a book he called *Illusions*. I first read it some two years after starting work on this book. I discovered that there is a strong similarity between the two books. Oh, his is written ever so much better. But perhaps that's because Richard is competent to have written it, whereas I am not competent to have written this one. Yet he made one terrible mistake. It's not really a mistake, mind you, but it might just as well be, because of the effect it will have on almost everyone who reads *Illusions*. At the very end of the book, right before the epilogue (yes, it, too, has an epilogue—isn't life strange?) he wrote, "Everything in this book may be wrong." When I first read this, the words hit me like a blow to the gut. Here I thought I had discovered a kindred soul only to see him slip behind a mirror at the last. He *had* to be kidding. In a way, he was. I came to understand those words eventually (I'm dense, and the spigot still drips slowly), but I do wonder how they affect others.

I shall not make the same mistake. Nothing in this book is wrong. Still, the book is not perfect. Don't be misled—there is a difference. Wrongness implies misinformation; lack of perfection, only missing information. In other words, this book is the truth but not the whole truth. There is surely some lack of information here. If I am incompetent to have written this book, then I am not competent enough to judge whether it tells everything it should.

No, quite the opposite.

Nevertheless, I state categorically that this book contains the one thing that is necessary. And what is that? The one thing that cannot be put into words. And how can something that cannot be put into words be contained in a book comprising nothing *but* words? That one's easy: The one thing needful is found in here disguised as words.

That's right—*disguised as words.*

Your mission, should you choose to accept it, is to put all these words together in the correct form. This will reveal to you the key. Should you choose not to accept it, that's all right too.

It will surely accept you.

Bear in mind the warning of Whitman's "Whoever You Are Holding Me Now In Hand" (see page 37). Take heed, lest you believe you have reached the innermost essence when you have merely scratched the surface. The Way is narrow, long, and hard, and those who find it are few.

Yet take heart. This little book holds the illusive *Secret of Life.* Beelzebub's grandson guaranteed it.

And so do I.

Notes for This Book

Here are a few notes to help understand what this little book is all about. If you found some things confusing or obscure, here is where you will find some answers.

General Notes

You will notice that the main character (Beelzebub's grandson) is never identified by name. This character is a stand-in for the author, and his description as given in the Prologue is essentially that of the author at the time the manuscript was first written (1979 through 1984). The character named Vadid is another alter ego for the author, and the reader will discover easily that *Vadid* is an anagram for *David*. Most of the events described in the book happened personally to the author, either as real events or as "head trips."

Prologue

The description of the location is accurate. La Cueva is now a part of the Las Cruces, New Mexico, park system. Many types of mushrooms grew on the north side of the principal rock formation; the allusion here is to those mushrooms that possess psychedelic properties, most of which grow in association with animal dung.

The part about Disney characters is an allusion to a type of blotter acid (LSD) that was popular in the area around 1979. The small squares of paper had a picture of Goofy juggling little plastic eggs. I counted these once and found there were exactly 46 of them.

The paragraph about the tape recorder is, of course, pure fiction. Beelzebub's grandson is simply my alter ego. No tape recorder was required to write these stories.

Chapter One

The protagonist's "bearded friend" is intended to be Baba Ram Dass (aka Richard Alpert, who was Timothy Leary's sidekick in the early 1960s). This chapter, like some others, has a poem or portions of poems by Walt Whitman separating it from the next chapter. Walt Whitman was one of Bucke's principal cases of cosmic consciousness; his writings in *Leaves of Grass* depict nearly every aspect of this higher form of awareness. The reader is advised to absorb these excerpts thoroughly.

Chapter Two

William Blake, whose words appear at the top of the chapter page, was another of Blake's primary cases of cosmic consciousness. The description in this chapter of what the protagonist observes while watching the "Seer" is a nutshell depiction of the author's own theory of nested universes.

Madman Muntz was a real person who sold television sets in the late 1940s and early 1950s. He also produced a short-lived sports car called the "Muntz Jet." I actually saw one of them on the street about 1952. More recently, there was a nice one on display at the Sarasota Exotic Car Festival in 2013.

Chapter Three

The quoted excerpt purportedly from the diary of Beelzebub (the protagonist's grandfather) is a verbatim quotation from the author's own spiritual journal for October 23, 1976. Once again, the theory presented in this chapter reflects the author's own belief about the true seat of consciousness of human beings.

Walt Whitman's poem "Whoever You Are Holding Me Now In Hand"—presented between chapters three and four as "Caveat Emptor!"—is a good depiction of the near-impossibility of transmitting the awareness comprising Christ Consciousness (Bucke's "Cosmic Consciousness") to another person.

Chapter Four

The description of Vadid—the anagrammatic "David"—given here once again fits the author at the time the manuscript was first written. *The Purloined God* is not a real book; it represents the beliefs of the author.

The description on page 42 of the "cousin" who freaked out is actually a description of what happened to the author when his son freaked out on an LSD trip one night. My first clue that this was happening was when my daughter came up to me and told me I should check on Dan, because he had just belted Frank in the face. Frank—not his real name—was another fellow who was considerably bigger than Dan. This seemed serious, but as reported in the book, it all turned out well (as those things usually do). It was not until a few years later that I finally realized that I had been the one who was "freaking out," as stated in the book.

The description on page 46 of the "older sister" is also taken from real life, but it was not a sister I saw walking toward me on the sidewalk—it was my own younger daughter. And she did not normally have a "dour expression" as described; it was simply that she did not look the same before I recognized her as she did after I realized who she was. And her face did "snap" into its usual aspect. The rest of the description is quite accurate. It *was* the first time I realized that the mental picture I had of her (as well as of other family members) might not correspond to the way other people may have perceived her.

Chapter Five

The reader may well glean from this chapter the author's belief that Shakespeare was saying more than he perhaps intended to when he wrote those words in *As You Like It*.

The description of feeling conjoined to the branches of a tree given on page 58 is again taken from real life. This actually happened to the author, but he was not under the influence of peyote at the time; rather it was from the effects of lysergic acid amides derived from Hawaiian baby wood rose seeds. It was a most peculiar experience.

Chapter Six

Lilith is the name of the "Eve" in the earliest incarnation of the "Adam and Eve" legend as taken from ancient writings of the Babylonians. She is presented here as a sort of prototypical woman, an iconic figure if you will.

I hasten to point out here that the sexual experiences described in this chapter happened to me only in my imagination. The first part of the chapter—up to the point where the protagonist falls asleep in the lean-to—is taken from a short story first written in 1975 as "Dione." It was not until I returned from a trip to the Holy Land in 1984 that I realized this story—with embellishments—would fit perfectly into the manuscript I was writing.

Chapter Seven

The references to Black Buffalo, Yellow Mouse, the place of "innocence," the "sees-far" place, and the medicine wheel are all taken from the book *Seven Arrows* by Hyemeyohsts Storm. Highly recommended reading.

The idea that the early books of the Bible were intended to be read and understood as allegory is not my idea. This principle and the dictum "Think Hebrew" are taught to prospective Bethel

Bible teachers, one of whom was my wife, Retta, who became a Certified Bethel Teacher. I learned these things from her.

The concept of the "dream agent" (page 81) was first proposed (so far as I am aware) by P. D. Ouspensky in his book *A New Model of the Universe* (New York: Vintage Books, 1971). Ironically, Ouspensky was a disciple of Georges Gurdjieff, a great mystic and teacher, from whose book *Beelzebub's Tales to His Grandson* I derived the title of this book as a play on words. An excellent discussion by Ouspensky on the concept of the dream agent can be found on page 254 of the Vintage Books edition of *A New Model of the Universe*. His full name is Peter Demianovich Ouspensky; his mentor's full name is Georgiy Ivanovich Gurdjiev; son of a Greek father and an Armenian mother, he was born about 1872 in Kars Oblast, which was then ruled by Russia.

The book *Cosmic Consciousness* mentioned on page 82 is by Richard Maurice Bucke, M.D. (originally published in 1900; reprinted in soft cover at New York: E. P. Dutton, 1969; reprinted in hard cover at New York: Causeway Books, 1974). It is subtitled *A Study in the Evolution of the Human Mind* and is the seminal work on the subject. Highly recommended reading. (The soft cover version is still in print.)

The two lucid dreams described on page 82 were both experiences of the author. The first one, about the sea monster, occurred sometime in the 1960s. It was the first lucid dream—i.e., one in which self-consciousness is attained—that I ever had. The second one happened about 7:45 a.m. on July 24, 1981; it so impressed me that I wrote it all down upon awakening. The actual dream sequence was much longer and more involved than the portion described in the story; only the most pertinent aspects are presented on page 82.

Chapter Eight

The reader should not be deceived into thinking that the entire text of this chapter reflects actual experience on the part of its author. On the contrary, only the material on pages 85 and 86—and exactly that amount, no more and no less—comprises my actual experience. The rest of the chapter is highly speculative on my part, but it is loosely based on some experiences of mine.

The incident described on pages 87-89 is pure literary invention on my part and does not represent even a distorted reflection of any real event.

The material on pages 93 and 94, beginning with the line "Before Abraham was, I am," does, however, represent some of my actual experience and thinking. Some of these things can be attained without achieving full Christ Consciousness in the sense that it is described earlier in this chapter.

Epilogue

Len Bias, mentioned on page 97, was a basketball player who died of a heart attack induced by cocaine use two days after he was drafted by the National Basketball Association. His case was a sensation at the time.

The statement by the late Peter Jennings was made in a special ABC network report "Drugs: A Plague Upon the Land" broadcast in 1988 with a very moralistic tone evident.

The facts related about Dr. William Stewart Halstead on page 97 were taken from the Consumers Union Report *Licit and Illicit Drugs* (Edward M. Brecher and the Editors of Consumer Reports, Boston: Little, Brown & Company, 1972). The facts in his case are indisputable and are presented in the Consumers Union Report on pages 33 through 35, where they easily can be checked by the reader. His description as the "father of modern surgery" is a direct quote from *Licit and Illicit Drugs* (page 35).

The book *Illusions* by Richard Bach is still in print (New York: Delacorte Press, 1977). I remark about the strange parallels between *Illusions* and my little book. Here is a good example. First, in the untitled preface (on page *v*) of this book, after stating "I did not want to write this book," I wrote:

> For years I went about my affairs trusting that tomorrow I should somehow come by the competence and knowledge necessary to write this book. Then one midsummer's night, in the wee hours of the morning, the Life Force of the universe grabbed hold of me and shook me until my brains rattled, telling me bluntly: "Tomorrow is Never!"

In Richard Bach's also-untitled preface to *Illusions*, he writes:

> I do not enjoy writing at all. If I can turn my back on an idea, out there in the dark, if I can avoid opening the door to it, I won't even reach for a pencil.
>
> But once in a while there's a great dynamite-burst of flying glass and brick and splinters through the front wall and somebody stalks over the rubble, seizes me by the throat and gently says, "I will not let you go until you set me, in words, on paper." That's how I met *Illusions*.

Now if that is not a spooky parallel, I've never met one. And I'll swear upon a stack of Bibles that I never saw his book before I wrote the preface to mine—or for that matter, before I wrote almost any of it save for chapters Six, Seven, and Eight. But you will find very little in common between those chapters—or this book—and anything in *Illusions*.

In the last few paragraphs of the Epilogue I hint at the real problem here. That problem consists of a basic conundrum: the mystical experience (for want of a better term) is ineffable: not capable of being expressed in words. That is why I write that the secret—"the one thing needful"—is disguised as words. The essence of the experience and the kernel truth of the Secret of Life is distilled into the words written in the book, but the reader cannot discern all of it simply by reading the book. It will require some triggering event in the reader's life before he can receive the complete revelation. It is not a thing to be grasped. This problem is well known by those who have experienced what Bucke called "the Brahmic Splendor."

That is the reason for the warning in the final paragraph of the Epilogue. Walt Whitman, who was himself endowed with a goodly portion of the transcendental awareness I call "Christ Consciousness," expressed this problem very well in his poem "Whoever You Are Holding Me Now In Hand," which is reproduced on pages 37 through 38 of this book. The reader would do well to absorb the meaning of this poem thoroughly.

After saying that it is all right if the reader does not accept this "mission," the reason I wrote "*It will surely accept you,*" is my hope that the things presented in this little book will sooner or later trigger an epiphany in the reader. In other words, I intended this book to be a catalyst. This is its hidden agenda. And that is precisely why the book is dangerous.

Whitman writes "The way is suspicious, the result uncertain, perhaps destructive" (page 37), and again "Nor will my poems do good only, they will do just as much evil, perhaps more" (page 38). Compare this with the words of Yeshua, who said "I come not to bring peace but a sword. ... A man's enemies will be those of his own household." (Mt 10:34, 36) *Caveat emptor,* indeed!

Despite all of this, the reader should not assume that the author is possessed of a full measure of Christ Consciousness as it is described in this book. The statement I made in the preface, "I've been granted but one small spigot that drips slowly, like a punctured tree trunk oozing sap," is still true today. But even a tree trunk oozing sap can eventually fill a bucket, as anyone who enjoys maple syrup is aware. I am very patient.

I have been to the top of the mountain and I have seen the Promised Land—I just can't live there . . . yet.